M

AND GOZO

SARDINIA

ITALY

SICILY

TUNISIA

Mediterranean Sea

MALTA & GOZO

LIBYA

HarperCollins*Publishers*

YOUR COLLINS TRAVELLER

Your Collins Traveller Guide will help you find your way around your chosen destination quickly and easily. It is colour-coded for easy reference:

The blue section answers the question 'I would like to see or do something; where do I go and what do I see when I get there?' This section is arranged as an alphabetical list of topics. Within each topic you will find:

- A selection of the best examples on offer.
- How to get there, costs and opening hours for each entry.
- The outstanding features of each entry.
- A simplified map, with each entry plotted and the nearest landmark or transport access.

The red section is a lively and informative gazetteer. It offers:
- Essential facts about the main places and cultural items.
  What is La Bastille? Who was Michelangelo? Where is Delphi?
- Practical and invaluable travel information.
  Everything you need to know to help you enjoy yourself and get the most out of your time away, from Accommodation through Baby-sitters, Car Hire, Food, Health, Money, Newspapers, Taxis, Telephones to Youth Hostels.

Cross-references:

Type in small capitals – CHURCHES – tells you that more information on an item is available within the topic on churches.

A-Z after an item tells you that more information is available within the gazetteer. Simply look under the appropriate name.

A name in bold – **Holy Cathedral** – also tells you that more information on an item is available in the gazetteer – again simply look up the name.

CONTENTS

CONTENTS

RED SECTION

Malta and her sister islands have been attracting visitors for thousands of years, lying as they do at the very heart of the Mediterranean, midway between Africa and Italy and halfway from Gibraltar to the Levant. All the great sea powers have fought over and ruled the islands, from the Phoenicians to the Greeks, the Romans, the Arabs, the Knights of Jerusalem, the French and finally the British, lured by the great natural harbours, the fresh spring water and the commanding position of Malta at the crossroads of empires.

The variety of the influences which have played a part in the islands' history has given them a colourful culture and a tolerant people. Like a carefully prepared dish, it is possible to taste a little Arabic in the language, a succulent tomato and some garlic in the cooking from Italy, a touch of Spanish in the architecture, perhaps some Sicilian in the dancing and singing. The fact that the islanders have been used to the British for nearly two hundred years, that they drive on the left and that practically everyone speaks English, makes Malta a remarkably unthreatening choice for many people while also offering a degree of exoticism.

Nowhere else will you find the romance of some of the greatest prehistoric temples in the world side by side with some of the earliest and most elaborate examples of Christian architecture; the grandeur of the capital Valletta which overlooks countryside still farmed by the wooden plough; the bright and cheerful fishing boats protected by a pagan eye on the bow – a wonderful anachronism in such a powerfully Roman Catholic country. The sum of these varied parts makes for a unique series of contrasts and mixtures which gives Malta its appeal.

Being so far south (the islands are on the same latitude as North Africa), the climate also makes for a superb haven from the north European winter, and the summer is predictably hot and cloudless. And as with all islands, the real fortune of Malta, Gozo and Comino lies in their sea, the warm and fruitful Mediterranean. Sited as they are, far from any populous mainland, these islands are in some of the cleanest waters of this sadly polluted sea. The west- and southwest-facing coasts are steep and rocky with magnificent cliffs at Dingli and Dwejra; the north and east provide startling natural harbours which have sheltered navies and fishing fleets, tankers and cargo ships, pleasure cruisers and yachts. The

fishing, swimming, diving and sailing around these coasts are second to none, although sheltered, sandy beaches are somewhat few and far between. Be prepared to get into the water from gently-shelving sandstone rocks and you will be rewarded.

The islands are almost entirely made up of limestone and sandstone, badly denuded, as is so much of the Mediterranean, following wholesale deforestation by early shipbuilders. The soft rock has been used in building for centuries, so the towns and villages, farms and field walls have always blended into the landscape – perhaps the name 'Malta' came from the Greek word for honey, *meli* (some say because honey from Malta was famous throughout the area, but could it have been because the whole island is honey-coloured?). The rural population is declining and much agricultural land is being taken up by developers, though the further you get from Valletta the more open the country becomes. Flocks of sheep and goats are a rarity now and if you ask a farmer if he ploughs

with a horse he will most likely laugh – practically everyone uses the 'mechanical donkey' now, an unwieldy vehicle driven by a small engine.

Malta became independent from Great Britain in 1964 and in 1989 made much of the celebration of its first twenty-five years of freedom. This is not surprising as it has been the only period of self-rule since before the birth of Christ! Politics is a serious business here and you will probably come across meetings and rallies, large open-air gatherings with impassioned speeches, flag-waving and bands.

For sixteen years the Malta Labour Party was in charge, trying to do its best for the workers, strengthening ties with Libya and turning away from Europe, often flying in the face of the Church. It was probably the latter which brought about the socialists' downfall. After a violent and bitter general election in 1987, the Nationalist Party took over

and is on the way to resuscitating the economy and reviving relations with the rest of Europe – animated discussion is taking place at the moment about whether or not to apply for membership of the EC. The island's major industries are based around the old naval dockyards in Grand Harbour – shipbuilding, refitting, repairs; textiles, clothing and other manufactured goods make up the bulk of exports.

Tourism is a major growth area and has galloped ahead in the last fifteen years or so, much of it aimed at the package-deal end of the market, although the tourist organization is currently trying to upgrade the image of Malta abroad. Without flattening some of the worst eyesores it is hard to know how this can be achieved, but the plan is to shift the emphasis from sun, sand and sea to the appeal of 6000 years of history. By virtue of its isolation Gozo has largely escaped the worst ravages of mass tourism, but there are signs of development here too, for example at Marsalforn. Comino has just one hotel, a few farms and very few acres, so it will likely remain as it is for some time to come. Another advantage, as far as visitors are concerned, is that Malta is extremely easy to get to, with direct flights from all over the UK and Europe, and ferries from Italy. The range of accommodation is also wide. There are umpteen package deals available plus private villas to rent, small locally-run guesthouses where you will get closer to the real Malta, major international hotels offering every facility, and self-catering apartments.

Malta has long been a favourite haunt of the British tourist and it is only fairly recently that

other European languages have been heard on the streets and in restaurants. The *What's On* guide now publishes details of the weekly attractions in German as well as English. There has also been little to attract the young in the past but the disco age has hit Sliema, St. Julian's and Buġibba and there is now a water fun-park along the coast too. Again, if glitz and other people are not on your list, head for the backwaters well away from Valletta, or go to Gozo where the pace of life is a great deal slower, there is very little traffic and the population is not falling over itself to find a space to build on.

Malta, Gozo and Comino have a lot to offer and it is up to you how to approach the choices. This guide aims to give an outline of the options, so that if you want to lie in the sun for two weeks you can find the best beaches, if baroque church architecture or Neolithic temples are your bag you'll have pointers, or if you want a little of everything you'll be able to find it all without too much trouble.

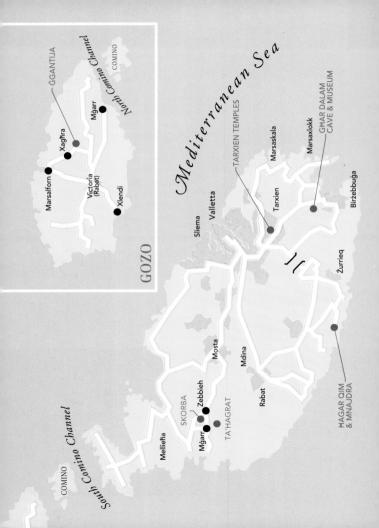

Mediterranean Sea

GOZO

GĠANTIJA

Mġarr

North Comino Channel

COMINO

Xagħra

Marsalforn

Victoria
(Rabat)

Xlendi

COMINO

South Comino Channel

Mellieħa

SKORBA

Mġarr

Żebbieħ

TA'ĦAGRAT

Mosta

Mdina

Rabat

Valletta

Sliema

TARXIEN TEMPLES

Tarxien

Marsaskala

Marsaxlokk

GĦAR DALAM
CAVE & MUSEUM

Birżebbuġa

Żurrieq

ĦAGAR QIM
& MNAJDRA

GHAR DALAM CAVE & MUSEUM Birżebbuġa.
❏ 0745-1400 Mon.-Sat. (mid June-Sep.); 0815-1700 Mon.-Sat., 0815-1615 Sun. (Oct.-mid June). Bus 11, 12. ❏ 15c, child 7.5c.
The museum contains the bones of extinct animals that once roamed the area. It is a short walk to the cave excavations where some of Malta's first inhabitants buried their dead around 5000 BC. See **EXCURSION 1**.

TARXIEN TEMPLES Tarxien.
❏ Opening times as above. Bus 8, 11, 26 then follow signposts.
❏ 15c, child 7.5c.
Some of the most astounding Neolithic temples to be seen anywhere, despite their modern urban surroundings. See **EXCURSION 1**.

SKORBA Zebbieh.
❏ Opening times as above (key from National Museum of Archaeology – see **MUSEUMS**). Bus 46. ❏ 15c, child 7.5c.
Huge stones mark the site of early temples. The wall and hut remains form the island's earliest known dwellings (4000 BC). See **EXCURSION 2**.

TA'HAGRAT Mġarr.
❏ Opening times and access as above. ❏ 15c, child 7.5c.
These two temples date from 3500 BC and have been partially reconstructed, giving a better idea of their original form. See **EXCURSION 2**.

ĠGANTIJA Xagħra, Gozo.
❏ 0845-1515. Closed hol. Bus 64, 65, 66 then walk. ❏ 15c, child 7.5c.
Hillside temples which are almost intact apart from their roofs and the images removed for safekeeping. The oldest free-standing structures in the world, according to the Guinness Book of Records. *See* **EXCURSION 4**.

HAGAR QIM & MNAJDRA Żurrieq.
❏ 0745-1400 Mon.-Sat. (mid June-Sep.); 0815-1700 Mon.-Sat., 0815-1615 Sun. (Oct.-mid June). Bus 32-35 to Żurrieq or Qrendi then walk.
❏ 15c, child 7.5c.
Copper-Age temples in a particularly striking setting overlooking the sea. Mnajdra has escaped too much rebuilding. See **EXCURSION 3**.

Mediterranean Sea

South Comino Channel

Marsaskala

Marsaxlokk

Birżebbuġa

BORĠ IN-NADUR

Żurrieq

Valletta

Paola

Sliema

Qormi

HAL SAFLIENI
HYPOGEUM

Siġġiewi

Naxxar

Mosta

Buġibba

Mdina

ROMAN VILLA
& MUSEUM

Rabat

GROTTO OF
ST. PAUL

ST. PAUL'S &
ST. AGATHA'S
CATACOMBS

Mellieħa

HAL SAFLIENI HYPOGEUM Burials Street, Paola.
❏ 0830-0915, 1000-1045, 1130-1215, 1300-1345 mid June-Sep.;
0830-0915, 1000-1045, 1130-1215, 1300-1345, 1430-1515, 1600-
1645 (Sun. till 1515) Oct.-mid June. Closed hol. ❏ 15c, child 7.5c.
*Extraordinary underground burial and temple complex believed to have
been excavated and constructed between 3000-1800 BC. The restricted
opening hours are due to the importance of atmospheric conditions. See*
EXCURSION 1.

BORĠ IN-NADUR Above Birżebbuġa.
❏ 0745-1400 mid June-Sep.; 0815-1700 Mon.-Sat., 0815-1615 Sun.
(Oct.-mid June). Bus 11, site signposted off road. ❏ Free.
*The remains of a huge defensive wall dating from 1500 BC are the most
remarkable of the site's attractions, but there are also a number of hut
circles, the remains of a temple and some 'cart ruts'. See* EXCURSION 1.

ROMAN VILLA & MUSEUM Museum Esplanade, Rabat.
❏ As above. Bus 80. ❏ 15c, child 7.5c.
*Reconstructed villa with mosaic floors, a marble bust of Tiberius and
household items such as lamps, glassware and beads. See* EXCURSION 3.

GROTTO OF ST. PAUL Church of St. Paul, Parish Square, Rabat.
❏ 0830-1200, 1600-1830. Bus 80. ❏ Free.
The cave where St. Paul (see **A-Z**) *is supposed to have taken refuge after
he was shipwrecked and before he was taken in by Publius, the Roman
governor. It has become a shrine where local people come for healing.
See* EXCURSION 3.

ST. PAUL'S & ST. AGATHA'S CATACOMBS St. Agatha Street
& St. Agatha's Lane, Rabat.
❏ St. Paul's 0830-1200, 1300-1800; St. Agatha's 0800-1800. Bus 80
then follow signposts. ❏ 15c, child 7.5c.
*A honeycomb of underground burial chambers, although there are no
bones or macabre remains. St. Agatha's are slightly smaller, but have
unusual frescoes and a little chapel dedicated to the saint. Not for the
claustrophobic. See* EXCURSION 3.

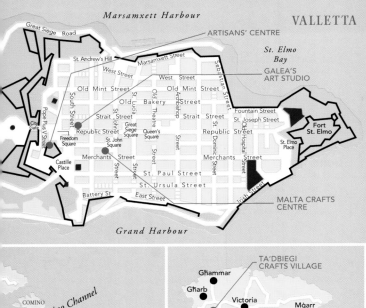
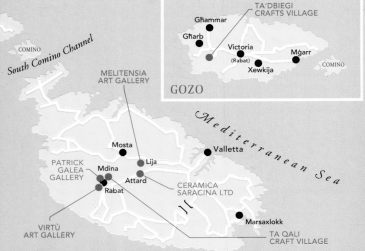

MALTA CRAFTS CENTRE St. John Square, Valletta.
❏ 0800-1230, 1400-1700 mid June-Sep.; 0800-1300 Oct.-mid June.
Good-quality textiles, glass, pottery, etc. See SQUARES.

GALEA'S ART STUDIO 70 South Street, Valletta.
❏ 0800-1245, 1530-1845 Mon.-Fri., 0800-1245 Sat. ❏ Free.
Artists' materials and competent local watercolours and prints.

ARTISANS' CENTRE 9 Misran il-Helsien, Valletta.
❏ 0900-1300, 1500-1900 Mon.-Fri., 0900-1300 Sat. ❏ Free.
Jewellery, glass, pottery, brass door-knockers – mostly mass-produced.

TA QALI CRAFT VILLAGE Between Valletta and Mdina.
❏ 0800-1600 Mon.-Fri., 0800-1230 Sat. Bus 80. ❏ Free.
Converted airfield huts where craftsmen are at work. See EXCURSION 3.

PATRICK GALEA GALLERY Palazzo Gatto Murina, Mdina.
❏ 1000-1300, 1600-1900. Bus 80. ❏ Free.
Prints, paintings, antiques and objets d'art. *Expensive but good quality.*

VIRTÙ ART GALLERY Villa X'Xemx, Buskett Road, Rabat.
❏ 1000-1230, 1600-1900 Mon.-Fri., 1000-1230 Sat. Bus 80, then 81
(ask to be put down by the church). ❏ Free.
Contemporary works by local artists among the villa owner's belongings.

CERAMICA SARACINA LTD 87/88 St. Anthony Street, Attard.
❏ 0830-1730 Mon.-Fri., 0830-1300 Sat. ❏ Free.
Hand-decorated plates, vases, plant pots, tiles, ashtrays and lamp bases.

MELITENSIA ART GALLERY Transfiguration Avenue, Lija.
❏ 1000-1300, 1600-1930 Mon.-Sat. Bus 40. ❏ Free.
Oil paintings, watercolours, prints, books and maps, all relating to Malta.

TA'DBIEGI CRAFTS VILLAGE Gozo.
❏ 0830-1230. Bus 1, 11 from Victoria (Rabat) to San Lawrenz.
Best for crochet, lace and woollens. Table linen orders ready next day.

GOLDEN BAY Bus 47, 52 to Għajn Tuffieħa.
Popular beach of soft sand at the head of a fairly open bay. There is a paying area (just as crowded), terrace café and plenty of activities, including windsurfing, pedaloes, boat trips to a nearby cave, sea-sausage rides (see CHILDREN) and water-skiing. See EXCURSION 2.

GĦAJN TUFFIEĦA BAY Bus 47, 52 to Għajn Tuffieħa.
Beautiful crescent-shaped bay overlooked on one side by one of the many towers which once protected this isolated part of the island, and on the other by dramatic rock formations. See EXCURSION 2.

GNEJNA BAY Bus 46 to Mġarr then walk.
Limited beach area compensated for by flat rocks ideal for sunbathing on the north side of the bay. The south side contains islanders' holiday homes and fishermen's caves. Lovely spot with lots of local colour. No café, but an ice-cream van in the car park. See EXCURSION 2.

GĦAR LAPSI Bus 89 to Siġġiewi, then Bus 94.
Swimming and snorkelling off the rocks is at its best here. Since this spot is a Maltese favourite, you may hear laughter coming from a shady cave where the women play bingo! The café sells excellent hobz bizet (see Food), cold beer and good-value sit-down meals. See EXCURSION 3.

PETER'S POOL Bus 27 to Marsaxlokk then long walk.
Glorious blue pool surrounded by soft shelves of sandstone; great for bathing. No facilities, so take a picnic. See EXCURSION 1.

ST. THOMAS BAY Bus 19 to Marsaskala then walk.
Almost pure white sand and ledges make this a popular bay. There are several cafés and the famous Fisherman's Rest restaurant (which has grown rather large, expensive and unfriendly). See EXCURSION 1.

MELLIEĦA BAY Bus 44 to Ghadira.
An extensive bay with a limited sandy stretch from Ghadira round to the Mellieħa Bay Hotel, dominating the northern shore. Amenities include water sports and a café. See EXCURSION 2, Ghadira Nature Reserve.

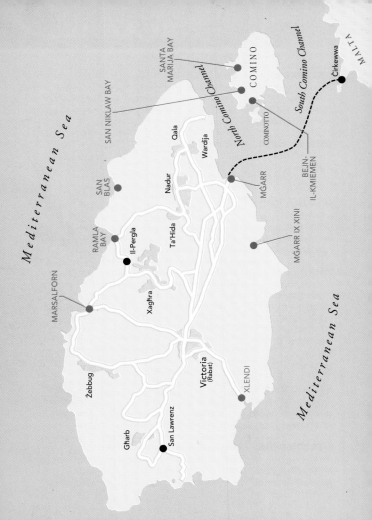

MALTA

Ċirkewwa

South Comino Channel

COMINO

SANTA MARIJA BAY

SAN NIKLAW BAY

North Comino Channel

COMINOTTO

BEJN-
IL-KMIEMEN

MĠARR

Qala

Wardija

MĠARR IX XINI

Nadur

Mediterranean Sea

SAN BLAS

RAMLA BAY

Ta'Hida

Il-Pergla

MARSALFORN

Xaghra

Victoria
(Rabat)

XLENDI

Żebbug

Għarb

San Lawrenz

Mediterranean Sea

RAMLA BAY Gozo.
Bus 31.
*Beaches are few and far between on Gozo, but this is one of the best
with its reddish, soft sand. See* EXCURSION 4.

SAN BLAS Gozo.
Bus 29, 30.
*About 1.5 miles north of Nadur, a rocky path through apple orchards
will bring you down to this sandy cove.*

MĠARR Gozo.
Bus 25, 26.
*Rather too near the town and harbour to be an ideal bathing spot, yet
convenient for a swim if you are in the area. See* EXCURSION 4.

XLENDI Gozo.
Bus 26, 87.
There is good bathing and snorkelling here from the rocks and ledges.

MARSALFORN Gozo.
Bus 8, 21, 22.
This tourist spot gets very busy in the high season. See EXCURSION 4.

MĠARR IX XINI Gozo.
Bus 25, 26 to Xewkija then walk.
This rocky but quiet cove is a long walk down the valley from Xewkija.

BEJN-IL-KMIEMEN (BLUE LAGOON) Comino.
On the northwest coast of Comino (see A-Z*), this is where the tripper
boats come in. The beach lies behind the tiny island of Cominotto in
fantastically clear blue water.*

SANTA MARIJA BAY/SAN NIKLAW BAY Comino.
*Both bays are for the private use of the guests at the Comino and
Nautico Bungalow hotels, but it is possible to use their facilities if you
book at least 24 hr in advance; considerable fee payable. See* **Comino***.*

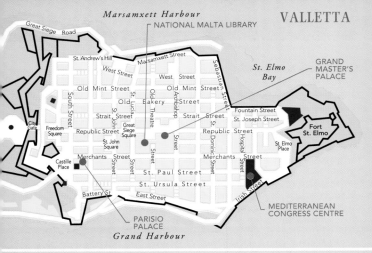

VALLETTA

Marsamxett Harbour

NATIONAL MALTA LIBRARY

St. Elmo Bay

GRAND MASTER'S PALACE

Great Siege Road

St. Andrew's Hill

Marsamxett Street

West Street

Sebastian Street

West Street

Old Mint Street

St. Lucia Street

Archbishop Street

Old Mint Street

Old Bakery Street

Old Theatre Street

Fountain Street

St. Joseph Street

Fort St. Elmo

South Street

Strait Street

St. John Street

Strait Street

St. Dominic Street

Republic Street

St. Elmo Place

City Gate

Freedom Square

Republic Street

Great Siege Square

St. John Square

Merchants Street

Hospital Street

Castille Place

Merchants Street

St. John Street

St. Paul Street

Battery St

St. Ursula Street

East Street

Irish Street

MEDITERRANEAN CONGRESS CENTRE

PARISIO PALACE

Grand Harbour

MALTA

Mediterranean Sea

SELMUN PALACE

Buġibba

Mellieħa

Naxxar

Sliema

Mosta

Valletta

PALAZZO FALZON

Mdina

Qormi

Paola

Marsaskala

Rabat

Siġġiewi

Marsaxlokk

VERDALA PALACE

Żurrieq

Birżebbuġa

GRAND MASTER'S PALACE Palace Square, Valletta.
❏ 0745-1400 mid June-Sep.; 0815-1700 Mon.-Sat., 0815-1615 Sun. (Oct.-mid June). Closed hol.
The archway from Republic Street leads into the tree-filled courtyards of this old palace, now the House of Representatives. See **SQUARES**, **A-Z**.

MEDITERRANEAN CONGRESS CENTRE Valletta.
❏ Shows every hr 1100-1600 Mon.-Fri., 1100 & 1200 Sat.
Originally the Hospital of the Knights of St. John (see **A-Z**), *it now houses the 'multivision show', The Malta Experience. See* **WALK 1**, **A-Z**.

NATIONAL MALTA LIBRARY Republic Square, Valletta.
❏ 0815-1315 Mon.-Sat. (mid June-Sep.); 0815-1745 Mon.-Fri., 0815-1315 Sat. (Oct.-mid June). Closed hol. ❏ Free.
Designed and built to house the Knights' archives. Note the bust of Dun Karm (see **A-Z**) *as you go up the front steps. See* **SQUARES**.

PARISIO PALACE Merchants Street, Valletta.
Napoleon stayed here during the island's brief period of French rule.

SELMUN PALACE Mellieħa.
❏ Ask at Selmun Palace Hotel for admission. Bus 43.
High on the Mellieħa Ridge, the 18thC palace can be seen from all over the north part of the island. Built as a fortified country home, it is now used for receptions by the adjoining hotel. See **EXCURSION 2**.

VERDALA PALACE Just south of Rabat.
❏ 0900-1200, 1430-1700 Tue. & Fri. (mid June-Sep.). Bus 81.
❏ 15c, child 7.5c.
One of the island's most impressive buildings, this moated palace was built by a Grand Master as a summer residence. See **EXCURSION 3**.

PALAZZO FALZON (NORMAN HOUSE) Villegaignon St, Mdina.
❏ 0900-1300, 1400-1630. ❏ Free.
A fine example of the style of architecture in fashion before 1530. The palace contains a private museum. See **WALK 3**.

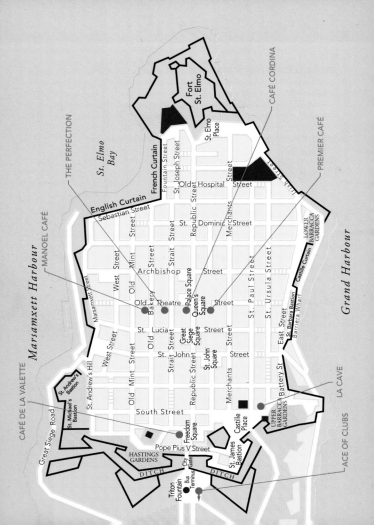

CAFÉS & BARS

CAFÉ DE LA VALETTE Misrah il-Helsien, Valletta. Corner of Ordnance Street and Freedom Square.
❏ 1000-1300, 1600-1900.
Good Italian ice cream, fresh doughnuts, an iced almond drink that is particularly thirst-quenching, and the ubiquitous cappuccino.

PREMIER CAFÉ Republic Square, Valletta. Next door to the National Malta Library.
❏ 1000-1300, 1530-1900 Mon.-Sat.
Long-established watering hole with an elegant atmosphere and tables on the square. Pastries and hot or soft drinks, or beer, aperitifs and snacks.

CAFÉ CORDINA Republic Street, Valletta. Opposite Queen's Sq.
❏ 0830-1400 Mon.-Sat.
Established in 1837, they play on tradition here – pink tablecloths, chandeliers, ceiling paintings by Giuseppe Cali and formal service. Wonderful ice-cream concoctions. Cheaper if you stand at the counter.

MANOEL CAFÉ 67 Old Bakery Street, Valletta. Opposite old Manoel Theatre.
❏ 0800-1330, 1600-2030 (later on Sat.).
Serves the best hot chocolate and almond slices in Valletta. A bar at one end also offers salads, toasted sandwiches and cheese pastries.

THE PERFECTION 56 Old Theatre Street, Valletta.
❏ 0830-1400 Mon.-Sat.
Take away or sit down – pizza slices, cheese pastries, coffee, etc.

LA CAVE Castille Place, Valletta.
❏ 1200-1445, 1830-2245 Mon.-Sat.
The island's one and only wine bar! Try the Maltese wine as imports are expensive. Serves pizza, pasta and salads. Live jazz Tue., Fri. & Sat.

ACE OF CLUBS St. George's Road, St. Julian's.
❏ 1900-0100. Bus 62, 67.
Cellar bar with pool, table football, video games; popular with the young.

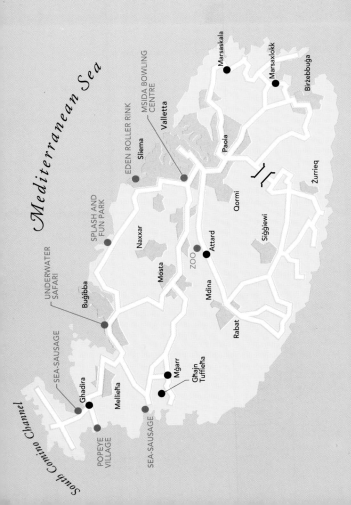

Mediterranean Sea

South Comino Channel

SEA-SAUSAGE

POPEYE
VILLAGE

UNDERWATER
SAFARI

SPLASH AND
FUN PARK

EDEN ROLLER RINK

MSIDA BOWLING
CENTRE

SEA-SAUSAGE

Ghadira

Mellieħa

Buġibba

Naxxar

Mosta

Mġarr

Għajn
Tuffieħa

ZOO

Mdina

Rabat

Attard

Sliema

Valletta

Paola

Qormi

Siġġiewi

Żurrieq

Marsaskala

Marsaxlokk

Birżebbuġa

CHILDREN

SPLASH AND FUN PARK White Rocks, Bahar ic-Caghaq.
❑ 1000-dusk. Bus 68, 70. ❑ Lm3, child Lm2 per day (includes umbrella and deckchair/sunbed); children's play park: adults free, child Lm1.
Water chutes, lagoon pool and bumper boats. Play-park area includes miniature trains, funfair rides, bouncing castle, go-karts, etc. Bar and café.

POPEYE VILLAGE Anchor Bay, Mellieha.
❑ 0900-1900. Bus 44 to Ghadira then walk. ❑ 50c, child 25c.
*Authentic-looking film set built for the Popeye movie. Attractions include a beach, children's play areas and dramatic cliff walks. You can also reach the village on horseback (see **Sports**). See **EXCURSION 2**.*

UNDERWATER SAFARI Il-Menga, Buġibba.
❑ 1030, 1200, 1330, 1500, 1630 & 2030 Tue., Thu. & Fri. Bus 49 or coaches from Sliema 30 min before departure. ❑ Lm3.75/4.25, child Lm2.75/3.25.
A specially-built boat giving clear underwater views of St. Paul's Bay.

SEA-SAUSAGE Golden Bay (Bus 47, 52) & Mellieha Bay (Bus 44).
*Take a high-speed trip round the bay on an inflatable sausage towed by a fast motorboat. See **BEACHES 1**.*

EDEN ROLLER RINK St. George's Bay, St. Julian's.
❑ 1400-2300 Mon.-Fri., 1000-2300 Sat., Sun. & hol. Bus 62, 67.
❑ Lm1.50, skate hire 50c.
Recently-constructed, colourful rink with capacity of around 800 skaters.

MSIDA BOWLING CENTRE Enrico Mizzi Street, Msida.
❑ 1530-2400. ❑ 10c, shoe hire 10c, games 40c (1530-1800).
Apart from the tenpin bowling alleys, there are lounge areas with American pool, video games and table football.

ZOO San Anton Gardens, Attard.
❑ 0700-1900. Bus 40 to Attard. ❑ Free.
*Unexciting collection of animals, including camels, goats and antelopes, but the gardens are lovely (see **EXCURSION 3**, **PARKS & GARDENS**).*

VALLETTA

Marsamxett Harbour

Great Siege Road

St. Andrew's Hill

Marsamxett Street

West Street

West Street

ST. PAUL'S
ANGLICAN CATHEDRAL

St. Elmo Bay

SANCTUARY BASILICA OF
OUR LADY OF MOUNT CARMEL

Old Mint Street

Old Mint Street

South Street

Old Bakery Street

St. Lucia Street

St. John Street

Strait Street

Great Theatre Street

Queen's Square

Archbishop Street

Strait Street

Sebastian Street

Fountain Street

St. Joseph Street

St. Elmo Place

Fort St. Elmo

St. Christopher Street

Pope Pius V Street

Freedom Square

City Gate

Castille Place

Republic Street

St. John Square

Merchants Street

St. John Street

St. John Street

Theatre Street

St. Paul Street

St. Dominic Street

St. Ursula Street

Republic Street

Merchants Street

Hospital Street

Battery St

East Street

Irish Street

ST. JOHN'S
CO-CATHEDRAL

ST. PAUL SHIPWRECKED

Grand Harbour

COMINO

South Comino Channel

GĦAMMAR

GĦARB

TA'PINU

Victoria

(Rabat)

Xewkija

Mġarr

COMINO

ROTUNDA
CHURCH

GOZO

ST. PAUL'S
CHAPEL

Mosta

ST. MARY'S
CHURCH

Mdina

Rabat

Valletta

Mediterranean Sea

Marsaxlokk

ST. JOHN'S CO-CATHEDRAL St. John Square, Valletta.
❏ Mon.-Sat. 0930-1245, 1500-1645. Closed Sun. and hol. ❏ 50c (inc. entrance to Mdina Cathedral Museum – see **MUSEUMS**).
*Vast church built for the Order of St. John, started in 1573. See **A-Z**.*

ST. PAUL'S ANGLICAN CATHEDRAL Independent Sq., Valletta.
❏ 0800-1200 Mon.-Fri.
The Cathedral's 65-m spire is one of Valletta's main landmarks.

ST. PAUL SHIPWRECKED St. Paul Street, Valletta.
❏ 1600-1800 Mon.-Fri.
*One of the city's oldest churches, filled with works of art. See **FESTIVALS**.*

SANCTUARY BASILICA OF OUR LADY OF MOUNT CARMEL Old Theatre Street, Valletta.
❏ 0600-1200, 1600-1930.
Damaged in World War II, but rebuilt. Light aspect due to marble pillars.

ST. MARY'S CHURCH Mosta.
❏ 0600-1000, 1600-1930. Bus 53.
*Round church with a dome reputed to be one of the largest in Europe. Its main claim to fame is the falling of a bomb through the roof during a service in World War II; miraculously it failed to explode. See **EXCURSION 2**.*

ST. PAUL'S CHAPEL Church Street, St. Paul's Bay.
❏ 0600-1000, 1600-1930. Bus 43, 44, 45.
*Grand Master Wignacourt added this chapel's porch. See **EXCURSION 2**.*

ROTUNDA CHURCH Xewkija, Gozo.
❏ 0600-1000, 1600-1930. Bus 25, 26.
The 75 m-high church dome vies with that of St. Mary's in Mosta for size.

TA'PINU Between Ghammar & Għarb, Gozo.
❏ 0600-1000, 1600-1930. Bus 61.
*The original church is now the Lady Chapel. A miracle tells of a demolisher breaking his arm when trying to knock it down. See **EXCURSION 4**.*

A one-day excursion to Paola and Marsaxlokk.

Take the busy Marsa road out of Valletta and follow the signs for Paola and Cospicua when you reach the main roundabout. The road goes uphill and you will see dockyards on the left and the new mosque (see **A-Z**) on the right. Turn right at the roundabout at the top of the hill.

4 km – Paola. Both the Tarxien Temples (see **ANCIENT SITES 1**) and the Hal Saflieni Hypogeum (see **ANCIENT SITES 2**) are near here. Leave Paola going towards Zabbar, passing the Hompesch Arch, named after the last Grand Master, and coming down to the sea at Marsaskala, a fishing village undergoing tourist development. At the head of the bay there is a sign off to the right for St. Thomas Bay.

10 km – St. Thomas Bay (see **BEACHES 1**). An excellent place to stop for a swim or snack. Return up the road towards Marsaskala and turn left in the direction of Żejtun. After about a kilometre turn left again towards Misrah Strejnu. Turn left once more at the chapel and follow the road to the end of the peninsula.

13 km – Delimara Point. A lighthouse stands at the tip of the point and there are excellent views over Marsaxlokk Bay. Drive a kilometre or so back along the road to a little group of buildings, one of which has a sign for Peter's Pool (see **BEACHES 1**). Turn down to the right where you will find a car park after a hundred metres or so of rough track. From here, walk down the path to one of the island's most beautiful bathing places. There is no café so you may want to take cold drinks with you. Drive north again, passing the prehistoric site of Tas Silġ on your right. Turn left at the church and make your way to Marsaxlokk.

16 km – Marsaxlokk. One of the most typical Maltese villages, largely deriving its living from the sea. The local market is excellent and very Maltese on Sundays (touristy during the week). There are good fish restaurants, bars and cafés on the quayside, from where you can watch the goings-on. Follow the road round the waterfront to St. George's Bay. Turn right, going inland, at the main junction and follow the signs for the prehistoric sites of Borġ in-Nadur (see **ANCIENT SITES 2**), Għar Dalam Cave & Museum (see **ANCIENT SITES 1**) and the remains of another Roman villa. From here it is only a short drive back to Valletta travelling north through Għaxaq, Tarxien and Marsa.

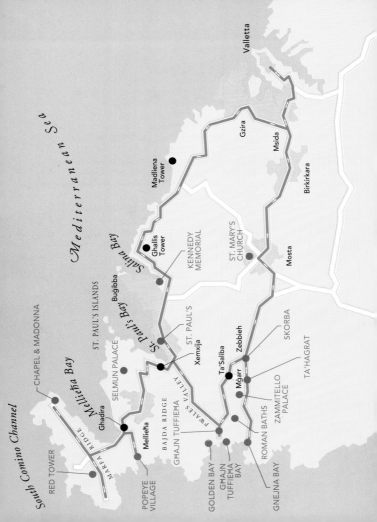

A one-day excursion to Mellieħa.

Take the main Msida/Gzira bypass out of Valletta and follow the signs
for St. Paul's Bay. Once you leave the suburban sprawl behind, the road
follows the coastline with its headlands marked by defensive towers.
20 km – Salina Bay. As you round the bay, you pass through a little
grove of trees with a sign to the Kennedy Memorial (see **A-Z**). The bay
was once famous for its saltpans, most of which have fallen into disuse.
The road then skirts past Buġibba which, today, is a busy tourist development. Take the fork to St. Paul's Bay.
22 km – St. Paul's Bay. Turn right opposite Connie's Fish Shop to get
down to the old harbour and waterfront, St. Paul's Chapel (see
CHURCHES) and an excellent coffee shop. Continuing on, follow the
curve of the bay, passing through Xemxija and on to the Bajda Ridge.
The road then descends into the Mistra Valley before climbing steeply
towards Mellieħa. Turn off to the right signposted for the Selmun Palace
Hotel, a new hotel which has been tastefully built alongside the old
palace (see **BUILDINGS**). There is a good view from here of St. Paul's
Bay.
28 km – Mellieħa. The town itself is not particularly exciting, but there
are a few good restaurants and, if you are ready for a swim, a sandy,
sheltered beach at Mellieħa Bay (see **BEACHES 1**, **Ghadira Nature
Reserve**).
Take the main road out of Mellieħa towards Marfa Ridge and turn right
at the top of the hill. The road is rather rough, but the chapel and statue
of the Madonna at the end look out over much of this northeast coast.
Return the way you came and when you reach the main road go
straight over towards the 11thC Red Tower (photography is strictly prohibited). At the point where the road peters out, there are spectacular
views down the west coast. On your way back to Mellieħa you might
want to take a detour to Anchor Bay's Popeye Village (see **CHILDREN**),
which is signposted at Ghadira, on the right. Take the main road back
to Xemxija and turn right through the Pwales Valley to Għajn Tuffieħa.
33 km – Għajn Tuffieħa. This is one of the most cultivated areas of the
island because of its rich soil and good water, and there are two beautiful beaches at Golden Bay and Għajn Tuffieħa Bay (see **BEACHES 1**).

Popeye Village

Carry on along the road to Ta'Saliba past the remains of a Roman bath complex (see **Ancient Sites**).

37 km – Ta'Saliba. Turn right in the village to reach Mġarr where the Ta'Hagrat prehistoric temples are sited (see **ANCIENT SITES 1**) – the key can be obtained from the National Museum of Archaeology on request (see **MUSEUMS**). Then drive down towards the sea past the fairly modern 'folly' of Zammitello Palace.

42 km – Gnejna Bay (see **BEACHES 1**). Little fishing huts, caves and boats give this attractive cove plenty of local colour. Take the main road back inland once more towards Zebbieh, passing through Mġarr again.

46 km – Zebbieh. The Skorba temples here (see **ANCIENT SITES 1**) constitute some of the earliest remains on the island. They too are locked and the key is available from the National Museum of Archaeology on request. The road back to Valletta takes you through Mosta with its famous domed church, St. Mary's (see **CHURCHES**).

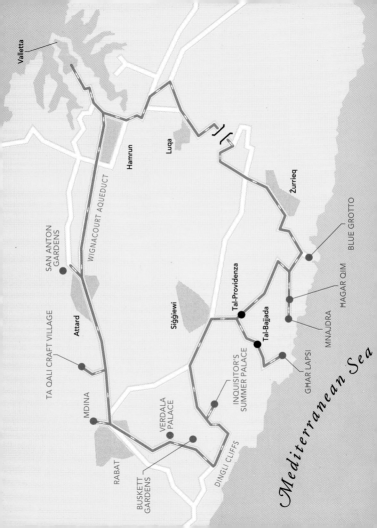

Valletta

Hamrun

Luqa

Żurrieq

SAN ANTON
GARDENS

WIGNACOURT AQUEDUCT

BLUE GROTTO

Tal-Providenza

TA QALI CRAFT VILLAGE

Attard

Siġġiewi

Tal-Bajjada

ĦAĠAR QIM

MNAJDRA

INQUISITOR'S
SUMMER PALACE

GĦAR LAPSI

MDINA

VERDALA
PALACE

RABAT

DINGLI CLIFFS

BUSKETT
GARDENS

Mediterranean Sea

A one-day excursion to Mdina, Rabat and Buskett Gardens.

Take the Rabat/Mdina road out of Valletta, which partly follows the Wignacourt Aqueduct, built in the early 17thC to bring water to the new capital.

9 km – Attard. Double back in the centre of town and turn off to the right, signposted to San Anton Palace and Gardens (see **CHILDREN, PARKS & GARDENS**). Return to the main road heading for Rabat and turn off to the right to the well-signposted Ta Qali Craft Village (see **ARTS & CRAFTS**) which is overlooked by the imposing Citadel of Mdina. Return once more to the main road and keep going in the same southwesterly direction towards the old capital.

14 km – Mdina. Park just below Howard Gardens (see **A-Z**) where there are plenty of cafés, and then take a walk around 'The Silent City' (see **WALK 3**). It is just a short distance from here to the town of Rabat outside the old city walls.

15 km – Rabat is a busy modern town. Attractions include the nearby St. Paul's and St. Agatha's Catacombs, the Roman Villa & Museum, and the Grotto of St. Paul (see **ANCIENT SITES 2**). Drive south out of Rabat, passing the Verdala Palace (see **BUILDINGS**) on your left.

18 km – Buskett Gardens (see **PARKS & GARDENS**). From the southern end of the gardens it is possible to take a walk, following the signposts, to the 'Clapham Junction' area. This is where the supposedly prehistoric 'cart ruts' run in all directions. Continue south on the road out of Buskett, which comes out above the spectacular Dingli Cliffs (see **A-Z**). At this point turn left along the coast and follow the road as it heads back inland, passing the Inquisitor's Summer Palace (see **A-Z**) on your right. Keep going in an easterly direction, bypassing Siġġiewi, and then turn right to Tal-Providenza. If you want to go down to Għar Lapsi (see **BEACHES 1**) for a swim and a bite to eat, take the right-hand fork after Tal-Bajjada and follow the road down to the sea. Otherwise, turn left and follow the signs for Hagar Qim and Mnajdra, some of the most beautifully-sited prehistoric remains in the whole of Malta (see **ANCIENT SITES 1**). The road continues down to the famous Blue Grotto (see **A-Z**). You can make your way back to Valletta via the villages of Żurrieq, Luqa and Hamrun.

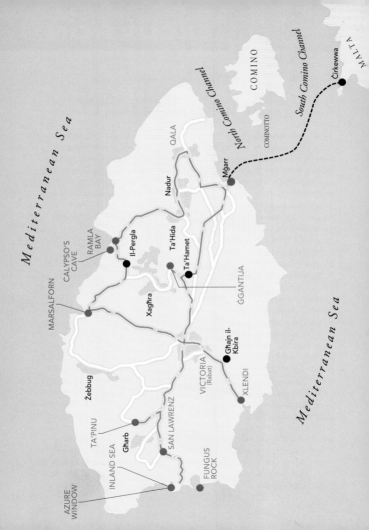

MALTA

Ċirkewwa

South Comino Channel

COMINO

COMINOTTO

North Comino Channel

Mġarr

QALA

Nadur

Mediterranean Sea

RAMLA BAY

CALYPSO'S CAVE

Il-Pergla

Ta'Ħida

Ta'Hamet

ĠGANTIJA

MARSALFORN

Xagħra

Għajn il-Kbira

VICTORIA (Rabat)

XLENDI

Żebbuġ

TA'PINU

Għarb

SAN LAWRENZ

FUNGUS ROCK

AZURE WINDOW

INLAND SEA

Mediterranean Sea

A one-day excursion to Gozo. It is advisable to take an organized tour but if you decide to take a hire car to the island, bear the following in mind. Ferry fare: car Lm1.75 (single), Lm3.50 (return); motorcycle 35c (single), 70c (return). There are few petrol stations, so fill up before you go. Otherwise, there are stations near the ferry in Mġarr and in Victoria. The roads are not good and signposting is basic. Take a good map.

Follow the road from Mġarr Quay (see **BEACHES 2**) up through the town, taking the right fork at the top of the hill towards Nadur. When you reach a T-junction turn right.

3 km – Qala. One of the last remaining windmills which used to pepper the islands can be seen here. Turn left in the town by the church, left again at the crossroads (signposted Nadur) and follow the road to Ta'Hida where you will see a sign for Ramla Bay.

9 km – Ramla Bay (see **BEACHES 2**). The beach here is of soft, reddish sand backed by a low green valley containing the remains of a Roman villa which is no longer visible. Above the valley to the west is a car park hounded by little boys selling prickly pear fruit, prepared to eat, which is very good. There are also old ladies knitting and a shop. The entrance to Calypso's Cave is a very narrow cleft in the rock. It is said that this is where the nymph kept Odysseus for seven years. As you leave the car park, take the road to your right through the village of Il-Pergla, turn right onto the main road and follow the hill down to the fishing village of Marsalforn.

14 km – Marsalforn (see **BEACHES 2**). This is one of the few places in Gozo which is feeling the effects of tourism. There are several hotels here, apartments are being built, and there are shops and cafés. However, the waterfront is still a lively place with fishing nets being mended, and the catch landed and sold. Take the main road out of Marsalforn for Victoria (Rabat) which can be seen clearly as you climb out of the valley.

17 km – Victoria (Rabat). The town's Citadel stands high above the surrounding, well-tended countryside, its honey-coloured walls mirroring much of the architecture of Malta. You will come into the capital by Capuchins Street. Turn right onto Republic Street and find somewhere to park. It-Tokk (see **MARKETS**, **SQUARES**) is on your left and

opposite you will find a narrow street (Castle Hill) leading up to the Citadel, or Gran Castello, as it is also known (see **FORTIFICATIONS**). The main gate will take you into the square with its Cathedral, the Law Courts, museums (see **MUSEUMS**) and Bishop's Palace. Follow the little street to the left of the Cathedral and you will come out onto the walls, with spectacular views over Gozo. On returning to the car, carry on along Republic Street towards the west, leaving Santa Sabina Square to your left, and taking St. Ursula Street out towards Għarb. After about 4 km there is a fork in the road for Ta'Pinu, the extraordinary basilica which has become a magnet for pilgrims (see **CHURCHES**). Return to the main road and take the next turning off to the left.

22 km – San Lawrenz. Turn left in the town and the road will take you down to the clifftops at Qawra for the Inland Sea, the Azure Window at Dwejra and to the south Fungus Rock (see **Dwejra**). All

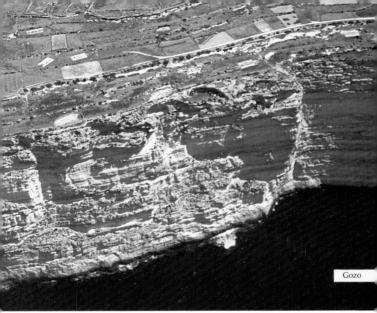

Gozo

roads radiate from Victoria (Rabat) so you will have to retrace your steps at this point to the capital, a distance of about 5 km. Return down Republic Street, take the first right after the Post Office – Main Gate Street – and follow the signs for Xlendi.

35 km – Xlendi. You will pass the old washhouse at Għajn il-Kbira on the way to this delightful village which has plenty of restaurants, and ledges from which to swim and relax for a while. Return to Victoria (Rabat) and turn right onto Republic Street. Follow this road for about 4 km, taking two left forks on the way.

41 km – Ġgantija (see ANCIENT SITES 1). The highlight of the afternoon, one of the best preserved and largest prehistoric sites in Europe. You will find the temples high on a slope facing south towards Xewkija with its massive parish church. Return to the road along which you came, turning left towards Ta'Hamet. At the T-junction turn left for Mġarr and the ferry.

CARNIVAL Valletta.
- Mid-February.
*Introduced by the Knights of St. John (see **A-Z**) as a final fling before Lent. Features dancing, fancy dress, and parades with floats and bands.*

FEAST OF ST. PAUL'S SHIPWRECK Valletta.
- 10 February.
*Fireworks are let off and homing pigeons released as the apostle's statue is brought out of St. Paul Shipwrecked (see **CHURCHES**) into the streets.*

FEAST OF ST. PETER & ST. PAUL Mdina & Nadur, Gozo.
- Late June.
The main festivities centre on Mdina and Gozo, though there is donkey and horse racing at Rabat in the afternoon.

FESTIVAL OF ST. GEORGE Victoria (Rabat), Gozo.
- Late July.
The highlight of the day involves horse racing down Republic Street, which used to be called, appropriately enough, Racecourse Street.

FEAST OF THE ASSUMPTION Throughout Malta & Gozo.
- 15 August.
Figures of Mary are paraded through the towns. Particularly splendid processions in Gudja, Mosta, Mqabba, at Valletta's Greek church, and Gozo's Cathedral (where it is followed by horse racing).

OUR LADY OF VICTORIES REGATTA Grand Harbour.
- Early September.
*Commemorates the end of the two great sieges of Malta, in 1565 (see **Great Siege**) and 1943, and consists of colourful dgħajjes races (see **Water-taxis**). Also celebrations at Mellieħa, Naxxar, and Xagħra, Gozo.*

FEAST OF THE IMMACULATE CONCEPTION
- 8 December.
*Although the feast day is celebrated everywhere, the festivities are at their most colourful in Cospicua (see **A-Z**), and at Qala on Gozo.*

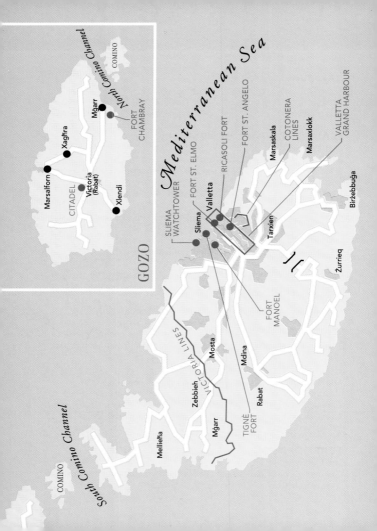

Mediterranean Sea

COMINO

North Comino Channel

COMINO

GOZO

Mġarr

FORT CHAMBRAY

Xagħra

Marsalforn

CITADEL

Victoria (Rabat)

Xlendi

FORT ST. ELMO

SLIEMA WATCHTOWER

RICASOLI FORT

FORT ST. ANGELO

Marsaskala

COTONERA LINES

Marsaxlokk

VALLETTA GRAND HARBOUR

Birżebbuġa

Valletta

Sliema

Tarxien

Żurrieq

FORT MANOEL

South Comino Channel

COMINO

Mellieħa

VICTORIA LINES

Żebbieħ

Mosta

Mdina

Rabat

TIGNÉ FORT

Mġarr

VALLETTA GRAND HARBOUR
Grand Harbour itself is dominated by the huge forts of Ricasoli, St. Angelo and St. Elmo, and guarded by Elmo lighthouse. Round to the north, Tignè Fort and Fort Manoel loom over Marsamxett Harbour (see **WALK 2**). *Stroll round the ramparts (see* **WALK 1**) *for a closer look or take a harbour cruise (see* **Boat Trips**). *See* **Valletta**.

COTONERA LINES Bus 1, 2, 4, 6.
These walls were erected as the outer defences of Senglea, Vittoriosa and Cospicua (see **A-Z**) *by Grand Master Nicholas Cotoner in the aftermath of the Great Siege (see* **A-Z**) *when the Turks made their final attack from this direction.*

VICTORIA LINES Bus 54, 55.
This wall, following the line of a fault running across the island, was constructed in 1897, under British rule, to defend the capital from any invasion from the north of the island. Just outside Mosta the road passes through the defences and drops down into the valley below. Pause in the gardens, from which there are extensive views (see **PARKS & GARDENS**).

SLIEMA WATCHTOWER Bus 60, 61, 62, 63, 64.
One of the small squarish towers built, mostly in the 17thC, on every headland as part of the coastal defence system. This one was erected by Grand Master de Redin between 1657-60.

CITADEL Victoria (Rabat), Gozo.
The medieval walls of this hilltop stronghold gave way to the Turks in 1551 and were eventually rebuilt by the Knights (see **A-Z**). *One of the island's highest points, they offer spectacular views. Walk up Castle Hill and enter by the main gate in front of the Cathedral, Bishop's Palace, Law Courts and the Knights' Armoury (see* **A-Z**). *See* **EXCURSION 4**.

FORT CHAMBRAY Mġarr, Gozo. Bus 25, 26.
One of the last of the Knights' great fortifications looks out over the harbour of Mġarr and the Gozo Channel towards Malta. It now houses a mental hospital.

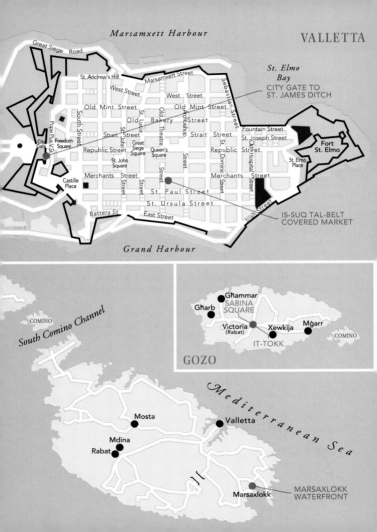

MARKETS

MERCHANTS STREET Valletta.
❏ 0830-1230 Mon.-Sat.
Everything from plastic buckets to jeans and costume jewellery, cheap souvenirs, tablecloths, cassettes and leather goods.

CITY GATE TO ST. JAMES DITCH Valletta.
❏ 0800-1600 Sun.
Always packed with Maltese families, visiting Libyans and Africans, and European tourists. You can buy anything here, including exotic antiques, caged birds, puppies, cakes, turtle shells, cloth, carpets, rosaries and goldfish, as well as locally-made jeans and T-shirts. See **WALK 1**.

IS-SUQ TAL-BELT COVERED MARKET Merchants St, Valletta.
❏ 0700-1400 Mon.-Thu. & Sat., 0700-1900 Fri.
Lovely old Victorian market building badly damaged in World War II (see **A-Z**) *and only recently restored and reopened. The shops offer some of the freshest meat and fish to be found in the capital, and several great delicatessens sell little round sheep's-milk cheeses, olives, Italian sausage, fresh salads, etc.*

MARSAXLOKK WATERFRONT
❏ 0830-1800 Mon.-Fri., 0800-1600 Sun. Bus 27.
Touristy weekday market where you will find reasonably-priced, locally-made table linen, hand-knitted sweaters and cotton clothing. In contrast, the Sunday market has an entirely authentic Maltese atmosphere and you will see a wealth of fresh fish straight off the boats on offer.

IT-TOKK (INDEPENDENCE SQUARE) Victoria (Rabat), Gozo.
❏ 0830-1230 Mon.-Sat.
Stalls selling fresh produce, fish and other foods, as well as clothes. Plenty of local colour. See **EXCURSION 4**, **SQUARES**.

SABINA SQUARE Victoria (Rabat), Gozo.
❏ 0800-1400 Sun.
Another excuse for a trip into town and a magnet for the whole island! Just up the road from the weekday site (see above).

VALLETTA

Marsamxett Harbour

Great Siege Road

St. Andrew's Hill

Marsamxett Street

West Street

NATIONAL MUSEUM
OF ARCHAEOLOGY

West Street

Sebastian Street

St. Elmo Bay

WAR MUSEUM

Old Mint Street

Old Mint Street

Old Bakery Street

Archbishop Street

Fountain Street

St. Joseph Street

Fort
St. Elmo

South Street

St. Lucia Street

St. John Street

Strait Street

Old Theatre Street

Strait Street

St. Paul Street

St. Dominic Street

St. Elmo Place

City Gate

Pope Pius V Street

Freedom Square

Republic Street

Great Siege Square

Queen's Square

Republic Street

Hospital Street

Castille Place

Merchants Street

St. John Square

Merchants Street

Irish Street

ST. JOHN'S
CO-CATHEDRAL
MUSEUM & ORATORY

Battery St

East Street

St. Ursula Street

St. Paul Street

Grand Harbour

COMINO

South Comino Channel

GOZO MUSEUM
OF ARCHAEOLOGY

FOLKLORE
MUSEUM

Għammar

Għarb

Victoria
(Rabat)

Xewkija

Mġarr

COMINO

GOZO

GOZO HERITAGE

Mediterranean Sea

MUSEUM OF
NATURAL HISTORY

Mosta

CATHEDRAL
MUSEUM

Rabat

Mdina

Valletta

Marsaxlokk

NATIONAL MUSEUM OF ARCHAEOLOGY Auberge de Provence, Republic Street, Valletta.
❑ 0745-1345 mid June-Sep.; 0815-1645 Mon.-Fri., 0815-1600 Sun. (Oct.-mid June). Closed hol. ❑ 15c, child 7.5c.
Houses the islands' prehistoric finds. See **Ancient Sites**, **Auberges**.

WAR MUSEUM Fort St. Elmo, Valletta.
❑ 0830-1330 mid June-Sep.; 0830-1300, 1400-1600 Oct.-mid June. Closed hol. ❑ 15c, child 7.5c.
Houses the George Cross awarded in 1942. See WALK 1, **World War II**.

ST. JOHN'S CO-CATHEDRAL MUSEUM & ORATORY Valletta.
❑ 0930-1245, 1500-1645 Mon.-Fri. ❑ 50c; oratory only 15c.
Flemish tapestries based on paintings by Poussin and Rubens. See **A-Z**.

CATHEDRAL MUSEUM Mdina.
❑ 0900-1300, 1330-1700 Mon.-Sat. (June-Sep.); 0900-1300, 1330-1630 Mon.-Sat. (Oct.-June). Closed hol. & 10 Feb. ❑ 50c.
11thC gospels, Inquisition archives, Dürer woodcuts. See WALK 3.

MUSEUM OF NATURAL HISTORY Vilhena Palace, Mdina.
❑ 0745-1400 mid June-Sep.; 0815-1700 Mon.-Fri., 0815-1615 Sun. (Oct.-mid June). Closed hol. Bus 80. ❑ 15c, child 7.5c.
Displays on Malta's geology and extinct fauna and bird life. See WALK 3.

GOZO MUSEUM OF ARCHAEOLOGY Citadel, Victoria (Rabat).
❑ 0845-1515. Closed hol. ❑ 15c.
Ġgantija relics, and Arab, Byzantine and Roman finds. See EXCURSION 4.

FOLKLORE MUSEUM Citadel, Victoria (Rabat), Gozo.
❑ 0845-1515. Closed hol. ❑ 15c.
Domestic tools and Gozo life style displays. See EXCURSION 4.

GOZO HERITAGE Mġarr Road, Għajnsielem, Gozo.
❑ 1000-1700. ❑ Lm1.50, child 75c.
7000 years of Malta's history in sound and vision – a real extravaganza!

STYX II

EDEN
PALLADIUM

St. Andrew's Rd

DEWDROPS

ST. JULIAN'S

Dragonara Rd

St. Georges Rd

AXIS

DRAGONARA PALACE
CASINO

PACEVILLE

Mediterranean
Sea

CAPTAIN MORGAN'S
PARTY NIGHT AT SEA

St. Julian's Bay

Grenfell Street

Lapsi St

Birkikara Hill

Balluta
Bay

Main Street

Sir Adrian Dingli St

Tower Road

SLIEMA

Sliema Regional Road

Manoel Dimech Rd

Randolphe

Strada Street

The Strand

Tower Road

VIBES

GZIRA

Sliema Rd

Sliema Rd

D'Argens Road

Marina Street

Sliema Creek

Dragut
Point

PALAZZO
CONSTANZO
FOLK NIGHT

Sliema Regional Rd

Testaferrata St

Ta'Xbiex Seafront

MANOEL
ISLAND

Fort
Manoel

Lazzaretto Creek

Marsamxett Harbour

VALLETTA

TA'XBIEX

Ta'Xbiex Seafront

Marina Street

Msida Creek

PIETÀ

Pietà Creek

Sa Maison Rd

Bus
Terminus

FLORIANA

MSIDA

Gwardamanga Hill

Wenzu Road

St. Anne Street

Grand Harbour

DRAGONARA PALACE CASINO St. Julian's.
❑ 2000-0400. Bus 62, 67.
Converted palace with an elegant, expensive restaurant. You can play blackjack, French and American roulette and baccarat.

AXIS St. George's Road, St. Julian's.
❑ 1900-0400. Bus 62, 67. ❑ Lm1 until 2230, Lm2 thereafter.
Big, modern disco with a good light show and bars selling expensive drinks. The place of the moment. Show at 2230.

EDEN PALLADIUM St. George's Bay, St. Julian's.
❑ 2130-0400 Tue.-Sun. Bus 62, 67. ❑ Lm3-4.50 (depends on artistes).
Great nightclub. Resident band and cabaret (2300-0100). No jeans.

STYX II St. George's Bay, St. Julian's. Below Eden Beach Hotel.
❑ 2130-0200 Mon.-Thu., 1900-0400 Fri.-Sat. Bus 62, 67. ❑ Lm1 until 2230, Lm2 thereafter.
Second most popular disco with locals and visiting teenagers alike. Usually packed. Floor show at 2300.

CAPTAIN MORGAN'S PARTY NIGHT AT SEA
❑ 1900-2400 Tue. ❑ Lm6.50 (inc. transport from hotel to Sliema quay).
Enjoy a buffet with wine, a disco and lots of party games.

DEWDROPS Ball Street, Paceville.
❑ 2130-0200. Bus 62, 67. ❑ Lm1 until 2230, Lm2 thereafter.
Disco attracting the twenties and thirties crowd. Mid-evening show.

PALAZZO CONSTANZO FOLK NIGHT Villegaignon St, Mdina.
❑ 2000 Fri. Bus 80. ❑ Lm5, child Lm3.50.
Includes a meal from an extensive menu, wine and folk bands. See **WALK 3**.

VIBES San Gwann.
❑ 2130-0200. Bus 41, 65. ❑ Lm1 until 2230, Lm2 thereafter.
Another disco favoured by a slightly older clientele. This time away from the Paceville heart of things.

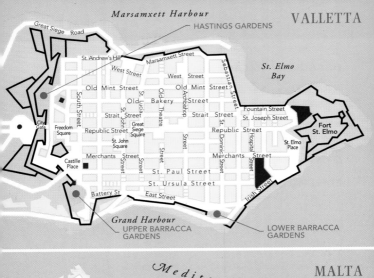

VALLETTA

Marsamxett Harbour

HASTINGS GARDENS

Great Siege Road

St. Andrew's Hill
Marsamxett Street

West Street
West Street

Old Mint Street
Old Mint Street

St. Lucia Street
Old Bakery Street
Archbishop Street

Sebastian Street

St. Elmo Bay

Fountain Street
St. Joseph Street

Fort St. Elmo

Strait Street
Strait Street

City Gate

Freedom Square

Republic Street
Great Siege Square
Republic Street

St. Dominic Street

Hospital Street

St. Elmo Place

St. John Square

South Street

St. John Street

Castille Place

Merchants Street
Merchants Street

St. Paul Street

St. Ursula Street

Irish Street

Battery St.
East Street

Grand Harbour
UPPER BARRACCA GARDENS

LOWER BARRACCA GARDENS

MALTA

Mediterranean Sea

GNIEN L-GHARUSA
TAL-MOSTA PUBLIC GARDENS

Buġibba

ARGOTTI BOTANIC GARDENS

Mellieħa

Naxxar

Sliema
Valletta

THE POINT GARDENS

Mosta

Mdina

Qormi

Paola

Marsaska

BUSKETT GARDENS

Rabat

SAN ANTON GARDENS

Siġġiewi

Marsaxlokk

Żurrieq

Birżebbuġa

UPPER BARRACCA GARDENS Valletta.
❏ 0700-2200. ❏ Free.
Peaceful spot near Merchants Street with stunning views of upper Grand Harbour. Statue of children by Maltese sculptor, Sciortino. See WALK 1.

LOWER BARRACCA GARDENS Valletta.
❏ 0700-2200. ❏ Free.
Situated at the city's southern extremity and offering stupendous views over Grand Harbour and across to Vittoriosa and Senglea. See WALK 1.

HASTINGS GARDENS Valletta.
❏ 0700-1900. ❏ Free.
Named after the first Marquis of Hastings, who is buried here. See WALK 1.

ARGOTTI BOTANIC GARDENS Floriana. On outer defences.
❏ 0700-30 min before dusk. ❏ Free.
Cacti and unusual plants, many with gorgeous blooms. See **Floriana**.

THE POINT GARDENS Senglea.
❏ 0700-1900. Bus 3. ❏ Free.
Last remains of a pleasure park built by Grand Master Juan de Homedes.

SAN ANTON GARDENS Attard.
❏ 0700-1900. Bus 40. ❏ Free.
One of the prettiest gardens on the island – fountains, rare trees, exotic shrubs, ducks and black swans. See **CHILDREN, EXCURSION 3, Music**.

BUSKETT GARDENS South of Rabat.
❏ 0700-1900 (later for special events). Bus 81. ❏ Free.
Orange and lemon trees, palms and holm oaks. The open-air theatre offers a programme of summer events including the Mnarja Festival (see **Events**). *See* EXCURSION 3.

GNIEN L-GHARUSA TAL-MOSTA PUBLIC GARDENS Mosta.
By gap in Victoria Lines where road climbs to Mosta. Bus 53. ❏ Free.
Pretty gardens looking over the north of the island. See FORTIFICATIONS.

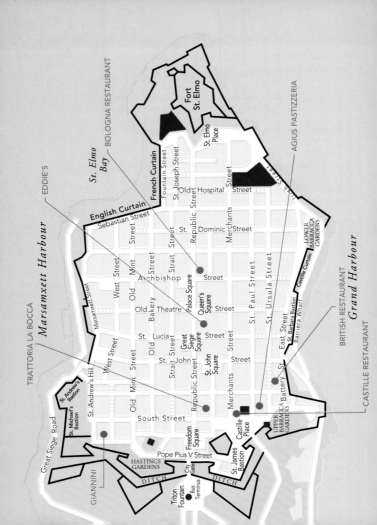

BOLOGNA RESTAURANT

EDDIE'S

St. Elmo Bay

Fort St. Elmo

St. Elmo Place

AGIUS PASTIZZERIA

Marsamxett Harbour

French Curtain

St. Joseph Street

Old Hospital

Street

LOWER BARRACCA GARDENS

English Curtain

Sebastian Street

Fountain Street

St. Dominic

Merchants Street

Castille Curtain

TRATTORIA LA BOCCA

West Street

Old Mint Street

Strait Street

Archbishop Street

Republic Street

St. Paul Street

St. Ursula Street

Queen's Square

Street

BRITISH RESTAURANT

Grand Harbour

Old Bakery Street

Palace Square

Old Theatre Street

Great Siege Square

Street

Street

Marsamxett Street

Barriera Wharf

St. Barbara Bastion

East Street

CASTILLE RESTAURANT

St. Lucia Street

St. John Street

St. John Square

Strait Street

Merchants Street

East Street

St. Barbara Battery

West Street

Old Mint Street

Republic Street

St. Andrew's Bastion

St. Michael's Bastion

South Street

Merchants Street

UPPER BARRACCA GARDENS

Castille Place

Great Siege Road

Pope Pius V Street

Freedom Square

St. James Bastion

HASTINGS GARDENS

City Gate

DITCH

DITCH

GIANNINI

Triton Fountain

Bus Terminus

GIANNINI 23 Windmill Street.
❏ 1200-1430 Mon.-Fri., 1900-2230 Fri.-Sat.
Typical little Italian restaurant high on the ramparts looking out over Marsamxett Harbour (see WALK 2). Try the Parma ham and fresh figs.

BOLOGNA RESTAURANT 59 Republic Street.
❏ 1200-1430, 1900-2030 Mon.-Sat.
Italian restaurant with Maltese specialities on the menu. Good-value main courses include fish, veal with herbs, or pizza.

TRATTORIA LA BOCCA 56 Zachary Street.
❏ 1000-1500, 1730-2100 Mon.-Sat.
Cool pastel and marble interior. The à la carte menu offers Italian pasta, fish, meat and chicken dishes. There is also a reasonably-priced tourist menu.

CASTILLE RESTAURANT (in Castille Hotel), Castille Place.
❏ 1200-1400, 1900-2200.
A fully air-conditioned rooftop restaurant overlooking Grand Harbour (see FORTIFICATIONS) and the walls of the city. Fresh fish is served daily, and Friday night is Maltese night.

BRITISH RESTAURANT (in British Hotel), St. Ursula Street.
❏ 1200-1400, 1900-2130.
Remarkably good value Maltese and continental dishes, as well as a marvellous view of Grand Harbour (see FORTIFICATIONS).

EDDIE'S 9 Republic Square.
❏ 1000-2030.
An establishment with a bit of everything, including a cold table, pizzeria and patisserie. Cocktails are also available and there are tables outside.

AGIUS PASTIZZERIA 273 St. Paul's Street.
❏ 0600-2000 Mon.-Sat., 0600-1200 Sun.
Home-baked Maltese dishes served straight from the oven.

Mediterranean Sea

South Comino Channel

THE TUNNY NET

GILLIERU

MARINA PUB & PIZZERIA

IL MERILL

IR RIZZU BAR & RESTAURANT

Marsaskala

Marsaxlokk

Birżebbuġa

Valletta

Sliema

Paola

Żurrieq

Mellieħa

Buġibba

Naxxar

Mosta

FONTANELLA

Mdina

Rabat

Qormi

Siġġiewi

Marsaskala

BUĠIBBA

Dawra Street

Red Cod Street

Bay Square

Bay Street

Spring Street

VENUS

LA TRATTORIA

IDA LEO

Winter Street

Islet Promenade

Summer Street

St. Simon Street

St. Anthony Street

Gulju Street

Bognor Beach

Bugibba Road

THE TUNNY NET Ghadira Bay, Mellieħa.
❑ 1230-1330, 1930-2230.
Classy and expensive restaurant specializing in seafood. Lovely views.

IL MERILL 9 St. Vincent Street, Sliema.
❑ 1900-2200 Mon.-Sat.
One of the best spots for a real Maltese meal. Try the seafood pasta.

IR RIZZU BAR & RESTAURANT Xatt Is-Sajjied, Marsaxlokk.
❑ 1200-1400, 1900-2200.
Popular with Maltese families. The lampuki *is served simply grilled.*

MARINA PUB & PIZZERIA 12 Marina Street, Senglea.
❑ 1000-1400, 1700-1930.
For a simple meal beside the water this bar is friendly and inexpensive.

GILLIERU St. Paul's Bay.
❑ 1230-1430, 1930-2300.
Popular with the Maltese upper echelons. Seafood dishes and a balcony.

FONTANELLA 1 Bastion Street, Mdina.
❑ 0930-1900.
In the walls of the city. Home-made pastries and pies. See **WALK 3**.

VENUS Bay Street, Buġibba.
❑ 1830-2200 Tue.-Sun.
Spindly black chairs and pink decor. Excellent pasta, meat and chicken.

DA LEO 84 St. Simon Street, Buġibba.
❑ 1730-2400.
Away from the bustle of Buġibba, the menu offers cerna in season.

LA TRATTORIA (in Hotel Concorde), Triq il-Halel, Buġibba.
❑ 1200-1400, 1900-2200 Tue.-Sun.
A busy, good-value trattoria which serves pizza, pasta, seafood and steak. There are tables outside.

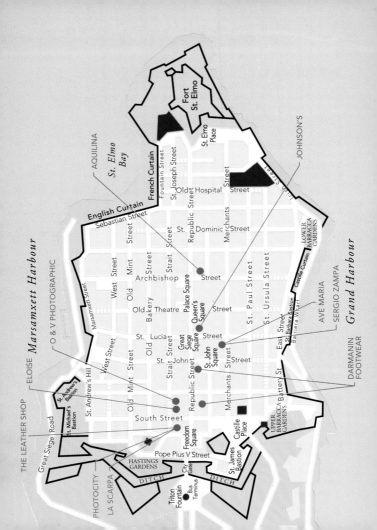

Fort
St. Elmo

St. Elmo
Place

AQUILINA

*St. Elmo
Bay*

French Curtain

Fountain Street

St. Joseph Street

Oldt Hospital

Street

St. Dominic Street

Merchants Street

JOHNSON'S

LOWER
BARRACCA
GARDENS

Castille Curtain

AVE MARIA

SERGIO ZAMPA

Grand Harbour

DARMANIN
FOOTWEAR

English Curtain

Sebastian Street

Republic Street

St. Paul Street

St. Ursula Street

West Street

Old Mint Street

Strait Street

Archbishop Street

Palace Square

Queen's Square

Old Theatre Street

Old Bakery Street

St. Luciat

Great Siege Square

St. John Square

East Street

St. Barbara Wharf

Battery St.

St. Barbara Bastion

Marsamxett Harbour

O & V PHOTOGRAPHIC

ELOISE

West Street

Old Mint Street

Strait Street

Republic Street

St. John Street

Merchants Street

THE LEATHER SHOP

St. Andrew's Hill

St. Andrew's Bastion

St. Michael's Bastion

South Street

UPPER
BARRACCA
GARDENS

Castille
Place

Great Siege Road

Freedom
Square

Pope Pius V Street

HASTINGS
GARDENS

St. James Bastion

PHOTOCITY

LA SCARPA

DITCH

City
Gate

DITCH

Triton
Fountain

Bus
Terminus

AQUILINA 58d Republic Street.
Bookshop selling dictionaries, newspapers, a good selection of books in English, and stationery supplies.

JOHNSON'S 146 St. Lucia Street.
The place for holiday reading matter, such as paperback thrillers and British newspapers (flown in daily). Also postcards, greetings cards, etc.

SERGIO ZAMPA 159 St. Lucia Street.
Good jewellery shop selling attractive silver and gold items.

AVE MARIA 161 St. Lucia Street.
Another good jewellery shop where you can find traditional filigree pieces (see **Best Buys***).*

DARMANIN FOOTWEAR 40/41 St. Zachary Street, Republic Street & Block 2, St. John's Square.
Reasonably-priced shoes comparable with Italian makes in quality.

LA SCARPA 64 South Street.
Well-made footwear in a wide range of designs.

ELOISE Strait Street.
Carries a large selection of leather and canvas handbags, wallets, beach-bags and suitcases.

THE LEATHER SHOP 12 South Street.
Beautiful leather clothes in the latest styles, both off-the-peg and made-to-measure (takes only three days!).

O & V PHOTOGRAPHIC 186 Strait Street.
Cameras, lenses, tripods, film, plus a processing service and a studio.

PHOTOCITY 57 South Street.
Offers a complete range of photographic equipment which should more than meet the average holiday-maker's needs.

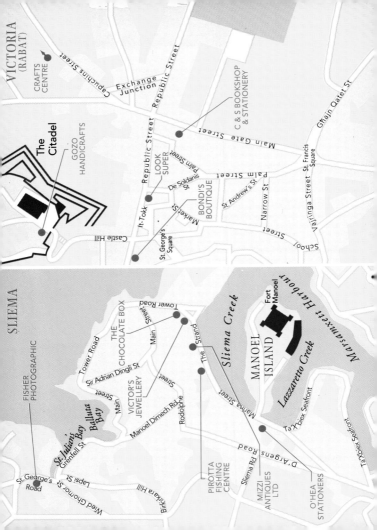

VICTORIA (RABAT)

CRAFTS CENTRE

Capuchins Street

Exchange Junction

Republic Street

C & S BOOKSHOP & STATIONERY

Main Gate Street

Ghajn Qatet St

The Citadel

GOZO HANDICRAFTS

Republic Street

LOOK SUPER

Palm Street

De Soldanis St

BONDI'S BOUTIQUE

St. Andrew's St

Palm Street

Narrow St

St. Francis Square

Vajringa Street

It-Tokk

Market St

School Street

Street

St. George's Square

Castle Hill

SLIEMA

FISHER PHOTOGRAPHIC

Tower Road

THE CHOCOLATE BOX

Main Street

Tower Road

Fort Manoel

Sliema Creek

MANOEL ISLAND

Marsamxett Harbour

Sir Adrian Dingli St

VICTOR'S JEWELLERY

Main Street

Street

The Strand

Lazzaretto Creek

St. Julian's Bay

Balluta Bay

Grenfell St

Manoel Dimech Rd

Rodolphe

Marina Street

Ta'Xbiex Seafront

St. George's Road

Lapsi St

Wied Ghomor St

Birkirkara Hill

PIROTTA FISHING CENTRE

Sliema Rd

D'Argens Road

MIZZI ANTIQUES LTD

O'HEA STATIONERS

Ta'Xbiex Seafront

PIROTTA FISHING CENTRE The Strand, Sliema.
Every possible item of fishing gear you might require.

THE CHOCOLATE BOX 19 Tower Road, Sliema.
Delicious confections to satisfy your sweet tooth.

VICTOR'S JEWELLERY 7 Tower Road, Sliema.
*Maltese filigree work, as well as a good range of gold and silver jewellery (see **Best Buys**).*

MIZZI ANTIQUES LTD 45 The Strand, Sliema.
Antique furniture, bric-a-brac and paintings.

FISHER PHOTOGRAPHIC St. Julian's.
A good selection of cameras, film and photographic equipment. Also offers a film processing service.

O'HEA STATIONERS 203 Marina Street, Gzira.
Maps, guidebooks, English newspapers and cards.

C & S BOOKSHOP & STATIONERY Main Gate Street, Victoria (Rabat), Gozo.
An outlet selling books, newspapers and a range of stationery.

GOZO HANDICRAFTS 38 Cathedral Square, Victoria (Rabat).
*A shop specializing in beautiful hand-made Gozo lace (see **Best Buys**).*

BONDI'S BOUTIQUE 2 Republic Street, Victoria (Rabat), Gozo.
All the latest women's fashions are available here.

LOOK SUPER 34 Republic Street, Victoria (Rabat), Gozo.
Both men's and women's clothes can be bought here.

CRAFTS CENTRE President Refalo Square, Marsalforn, Gozo.
Hand-made Gozo lace is on sale at this crafts centre situated on the island's north coast.

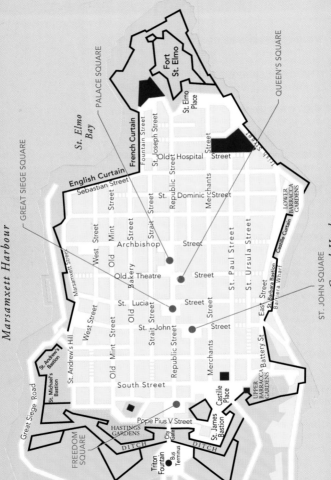

Marsamxett Harbour

Grand Harbour

St. Elmo Bay

PALACE SQUARE

QUEEN'S SQUARE

GREAT SIEGE SQUARE

Fort
St. Elmo

St. Elmo
Place

French Curtain

Fountain Street

St. Joseph Street

Old Hospital

Street

Street

LOWER
BARRACCA
GARDENS

English Curtain

Sebastian Street

Republic Street

St. Dominic Street

Merchants Street

Castille Curtain

West Street

Old Mint Street

Strait Street

St. Paul Street

St. Ursula Street

Archbishop Street

Marsamxett Street

ST. JOHN SQUARE

Old Bakery Street

Theatre Street

Street

St. Barbara Bastion

St. Lucia Street

Strait Street

Barriera Wharf

West Street

Old Mint Street

St. John Street

Merchants Street

East Street

Battery Street

UPPER
BARRACCA
GARDENS

St. Andrew's Hill

Republic Street

Castille Place

St. Andrew's Bastion

St. Michael's Bastion

South Street

Castille Place

Great Siege Road

Pope Pius V Street

St. James Bastion

HASTINGS
GARDENS

City Gate

DITCH

DITCH

FREEDOM
SQUARE

Triton
Fountain

Bus
Terminus

GREAT SIEGE SQUARE Valletta.

*A welcome area of shade beneath the Cathedral walls on Republic Street. The imposing, classical-style Law Courts stand opposite. This is one of the places where you can hire a horse-drawn karrozzin (see **A-Z**) for sightseeing.*

REPUBLIC SQUARE (QUEEN'S SQUARE) Valletta.

*Providing another break along Republic Street, this square, in front of the National Malta Library (see **BUILDINGS**), contains a red pillar box, a statue of Queen Victoria and shaded café tables.*

PALACE SQUARE Valletta.

*This square right at the heart of Valletta, now largely a car park, is surrounded by noteworthy buildings, including the Grand Master's Palace (see **BUILDINGS**, **A-Z**), the Treasury of the Order and the Main Guard. The latter is inscribed: 'To great and unconquered Britain the love of the Maltese and the voice of Europe confirms these islands AD 1814'.*

ST. JOHN SQUARE Valletta.

*A wide, open space in which to appreciate the massive frontage of the Cathedral (see **CHURCHES**, **St. John's Co-Cathedral & Oratory**) with its great cannon. A colonnade housing excellent shops, including the Malta Crafts Centre (see **ARTS & CRAFTS**), runs around the square.*

FREEDOM SQUARE Valletta.

*As you enter Valletta through City Gate, with Republic Street stretching away in front of you, you will see the huge bombed ruins of the Opera House on your right. The main tourist office (see **Tourist Information**) is to the right of the gate and you can gain access to the city walls from the corner on your left (see **WALK 1**).*

IT-TOKK (INDEPENDENCE SQUARE) Victoria (Rabat), Gozo.

*Rabat's main square lies at the foot of Castle Hill, just off Republic Street, which leads up to the Citadel (see **FORTIFICATIONS**). It contains the town's best shops and the tourist office (see **Tourist Information**). There is a colourful market (see **MARKETS**) every morning. See **EXCURSION 4**.*

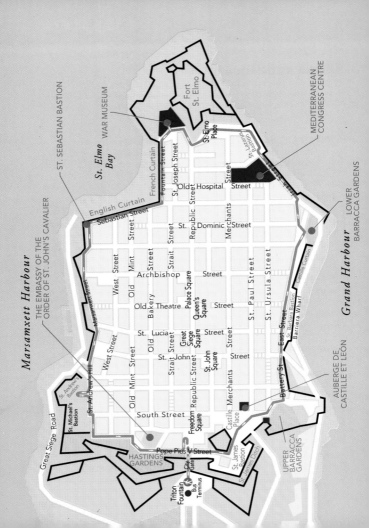

Marsamxett Harbour

ST. SEBASTIAN BASTION

St. Elmo Bay

Fort St. Elmo

WAR MUSEUM

MEDITERRANEAN CONGRESS CENTRE

THE EMBASSY OF THE ORDER OF ST. JOHN'S CAVALIER

St. Elmo Place

St. Lazarus Bastion

LOWER BARRACCA GARDENS

French Curtain

English Curtain

Sebastian Street

St. Joseph Street

Fountain Street

Old Hospital Street

St. Dominic Street

Republic Street

Merchants Street

Marsamxett Street

West Street

Old Mint Street

Strait Street

Archbishop Street

Grand Harbour

St. Paul Street

St. Ursula Street

Marine Curtain

Old Bakery Street

Palace Square

Queen's Square

St. Lucia Street

Great Siege Square

Strait Street

St. John Square

Old Mint Street

Strait Street

St. John Street

East Street

St. Barbara Bastion

Barriera Wharf

West Street

South Street

Freedom Square

Republic Street

Castille Place

Merchants Street

AUBERGE DE CASTILLE ET LEÓN

Battery St.

St. Andrew's Bastion

St. Michael's Bastion

Great Siege Road

HASTINGS GARDENS

Pope Pius V Street

City Gate

Triton Fountain

Bus Terminus

St. James Bastion

St. James Ditch

UPPER BARRACCA GARDENS

Valletta City Walls

2 hr.

As you enter Valletta's City Gate, turn left immediately and you will find stone steps in the corner which lead up inside the walls to the top of the fortifications and Pope Pius V Street. From this vantage point you can look, in one direction, right down busy Republic Street and, in the other, out over the walls to the chaotic bus terminus and the grand (and currently closed) Phoenicia Hotel across to Floriana (see **A-Z**). Turn right towards Grand Harbour to reach St. James Bastion, backed by recently replaced and restored cannon, which overlooks the Ditch, site of a Sunday market (see **MARKETS**).

Carry on to Castille Place, dominated by the Auberge de Castille et León, now the Prime Minister's office (see **Auberges**). The statue in the centre of the square is of Giorgio Borg Olivier, Prime Minister 1950-55 and 1962-71. Take the entrance to the Upper Barracca Gardens (see **PARKS & GARDENS**) beside the Old Garrison Church (now the Central Mail Room – red pillar box outside) for wonderful views of Grand Harbour and its defences (see **FORTIFICATIONS**).

Coming out of the gardens, turn right and walk down Battery Street to St. Barbara Bastion, overlooking Barriera Wharf and the old fish market far below. Continue on just beyond Castille Curtain to the Lower Barracca Gardens (see **PARKS & GARDENS**), another attractive haven of greenery and fountains, where there is an even broader panorama of Grand Harbour: the harbour entrance guarded by Elmo lighthouse to the left, Fort Ricasoli to the right, and Fort St. Angelo across the harbour at Vittoriosa (see **A-Z**).

Follow the walls north along Irish Street, passing the Hospital of the Order of St. John on the left, which is now the Mediterranean Congress Centre (see **BUILDINGS**, **A-Z**), just before you reach St. Lazarus Bastion. The granaries in front of Fort St. Elmo, just after this, are similar to those in Floriana – underground pits covered with stone lids. Visit the fort's War Museum (see **MUSEUMS**) to see the way in which the massive defences you are walking along were utilized in World War II (see **A-Z**).

Keep going in the same direction below Fountain Street and St. Sebastian Street and you will find yourself looking down on St. Elmo Bay, backed by first the French Curtain and then the English Curtain

(these great walls were never scaled by an enemy). When you get to St. Sebastian Bastion stop at the café for a cold drink and a rest, during which you can enjoy the magnificent view over Marsamxett Harbour to Manoel Island and Sliema (with Tignè Fort at its tip). When you are sufficiently rested resume walking along Marsamxett Street to the point it swings off to the right and becomes Great Siege Road. Take the narrow stepped street, St. Andrew's Hill, which leads up onto St. Andrew's Bastion. The view back towards the city from here is particularly lovely, especially in the early evening when the soft light illuminates the tall spire of

the Anglican Cathedral and the dome of the Sanctuary Basilica of Our Lady of Mount Carmel (see **CHURCHES**).

Walk from here back to St. Andrew's Street and on to City Gate through Hastings Gardens (see **PARKS & GARDENS**), named after a former governor of the island whose (noseless) figure reclines on his classically-styled mausoleum by the gate. There are firework displays in the gardens on special occasions. The cannon in the crenels overlooking Msida and Floriana have only recently been remounted on their original site. The Embassy of the Order of St. John's Cavalier stands on your left as you round the corner.

Descend into Freedom Square (see **SQUARES**) by the same steps you came up at the beginning of the walk.

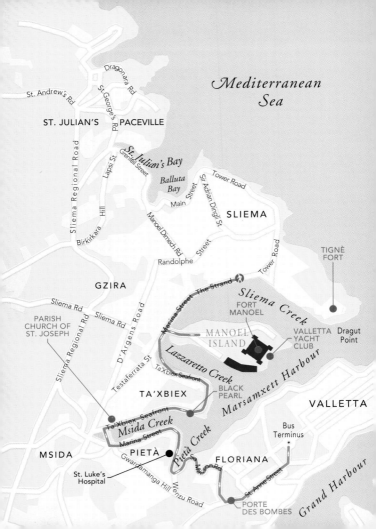

Mediterranean Sea

St. Andrew's Rd

Dragonara Rd

St-George's Rd

ST. JULIAN'S PACEVILLE

St. Julian's Bay

Grenfel Street

Lapsi St.

Balluta Bay

Birkirkara Hill

Sliema Regional Road

Manoel Dimech Rd

Sir Adrian Dingli St.

Main Street

Tower Road

SLIEMA

Street

Randolphe

Tower Road

TIGNÉ FORT

GZIRA

Sliema Rd

Sliema Rd

D'Argens Road

Testaferrata St.

Ta'Xbiex Seafront

Marina Street The Strand

Sliema Creek

FORT MANOEL

MANOEL ISLAND

VALLETTA YACHT CLUB

Dragut Point

PARISH CHURCH OF ST. JOSEPH

Sliema Regional Rd

Lazzaretto Creek

Ta'Xbiex — Seafront

TA'XBIEX

BLACK PEARL

Marsamxett Harbour

VALLETTA

Msida Creek

Marina Street

Bus Terminus

MSIDA

Gwardamanga Hill

PIETÀ

Pietà Creek

Rd

FLORIANA

St. Luke's Hospital

Vjenzu Road

St. Anne Street

PORTE DES BOMBES

Grand Harbour

Marsamxett Harbour & Creeks

2-3 hr.

Take a bus (60-64) to Sliema and get off at the main Strand stop to find yourself on the bustling Sliema waterfront with its hotels, bars, cafés and restaurants. Sliema Creek is protected from the sea by Tignè Fort on Dragut Point (see **FORTIFICATIONS**), which was named after the Turkish general who raided Malta in 1551 and who assisted in the Great Siege (see **A-Z**). Built in 1793, it was the last of the great defences built by the Knights of St. John (see **A-Z**). The creek itself is packed with rowing boats, small cruisers, brightly-coloured *luzzus* and pleasure craft (many of the harbour cruises leave from here – see **Boat Trips**).

Walk westwards along the promenade to the causeway onto Manoel Island, named after the Grand Master (1722-36) who oversaw the construction of the great fort which stands on the far side of the island (see **FORTIFICATIONS**). This is also the site of Valletta Yacht Club, the old 17thC quarantine hospital (the Lazzaretto) and the Phoenician Glass Blowers factory (reach it by walking round the boatyard or going over by their own, free, ferry – see **Best Buys**).

Return to the mainland and continue round the head of Lazzaretto Creek through the little gardens, past the children's playground, to the first of the large yachts moored here. There is a pretty church on the right and walled villas with cascades of bougainvillea.

As you round the corner from Ta'Xbiex to Msida Creek, you pass a huge ship, the *Black Pearl*, which has been built into the quayside and is now a bar/restaurant. Note the beautiful ocean-going yachts, mostly for charter, though some are still private, moored along this stretch. The Parish Church of St. Joseph stands beside the marina among the hotels and chandlers. Carry on to the pleasantly shady, south side of the creek and follow the waterfront path round past St. Luke's Hospital to Pietà Creek, a little inlet full of small, local boats. The boat shed on the far bank used to be an old fish market. One of the Gozo ferries leaves from the Creek (see **Ferries**). It was also the scene of an ingenious Turkish feat during the Great Siege: finding the entrance to Grand Harbour too well defended, the fleet landed here and dragged their ships half a mile overland towards Marsa. Either walk up through the pines and fortifications to Floriana (see **A-Z**) through the Porte des Bombes to the bus terminus or catch any bus back to City Gate.

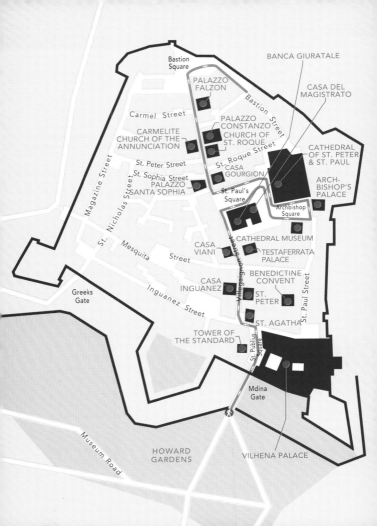

BANCA GIURATALE

CASA DEL
MAGISTRATO

Bastion
Square

PALAZZO
FALZON

Bastion Street

Carmel Street

PALAZZO
CONSTANZO
CARMELITE
CHURCH OF THE
ANNUNCIATION

CHURCH OF
ST. ROQUE

CATHEDRAL
OF ST. PETER
& ST. PAUL

St. Peter Street

St. Roque Street

CASA
GOURGION

ARCH-
BISHOP'S
PALACE

St. Sophia Street

PALAZZO
SANTA SOPHIA

St. Paul's
Square

Magazine Street

St. Nicholas Street

Archbishop
Square

CATHEDRAL MUSEUM

CASA
VIANI

TESTAFERRATA
PALACE

Mesquita   Street

BENEDICTINE
CONVENT

Whitegnaton Street

CASA
INGUANEZ

Greeks
Gate

ST.
PETER

St. Paul Street

Inguanez Street

ST. AGATHA

TOWER OF
THE STANDARD

St. Publius Square

Mdina
Gate

Museum Road

HOWARD
GARDENS

VILHENA PALACE

2 hr.

The ancient capital is closed to traffic (see **EXCURSION 3**) and therefore particularly pleasant to walk in. As you approach the city, high on a bluff almost in the centre of the island and surrounded by massive walls successively built and added to by the Romans, the Byzantines, the Arabs and the Knights of St. John (see **A-Z**), you will see why this site was chosen by Malta's earliest inhabitants as a stronghold.

Go through Howard Gardens (see **A-Z**), crossing the ditch (now full of trees and flowerbeds) dug by the Arabs to separate Mdina from Rabat and make the Citadel even more secure, to enter 'The Silent City' by Mdina Gate. The tower on your left (Tower of the Standard) now houses the police station, and the beautiful Vilhena Palace on your right is home to the Museum of Natural History (see **MUSEUMS**). Follow the green sign for the Cathedral Museum to the left, taking you on to the main thoroughfare of Villegaignon Street. Pause in front of Casa Inguanez, on the left, to look at the enormous knockers on the door of the ancestral seat of one of Malta's oldest families. Opposite, on the right, are the seemingly impenetrable walls of the Benedictine convent, and the churches of St. Agatha and St. Peter.

Continue walking in the same direction to St. Paul's Square, past Casa Viani on the left and the Testaferrata Palace on the right. Both are further examples of the well-restored homes of Malta's aristocracy. The Banca Giuratale, further along and also on the right, and the Casa del Magistrato behind it, in the square itself, were built as administrative centres around 1730. The square is dominated by the Cathedral of St. Peter and St. Paul, supposedly built on the site of one of the island's earliest churches and, before that, the villa of the Roman governor, Publius. With its pleasingly-proportioned facade and rich interior it is one of the best examples of baroque church architecture to be found on Malta. Many of the Cathedral treasures are displayed in the Old Seminary across Bishop Square and in the Cathedral Museum (see **MUSEUMS**), including a notable coin collection, works by Dürer, Rembrandt, Goya and Van Dyck, illuminated manuscripts and silverware. The Archbishop's Palace stands next door and to the right of the Cathedral. Return to Villegaignon Street and carry on walking in the same direction.

The Palazzo Santa Sophia, on your left, is said to be one of the oldest buildings on Malta and dates from about 1230. The Casa Gourgion stands opposite it, and the Church of St. Roque occupies the next corner. Across from it is the Carmelite Church of the Annunciation. The next palace you come to is the Palazzo Constanzo which is now a hotel and restaurant (see **NIGHTLIFE**). Near the end of the street you come to the Palazzo Falzon (see **BUILDINGS**), also known as the Norman House, containing a private museum. Just past this is the northernmost bastion of the city, where there is a magnificent

view over the Maltese countryside to Mtarfa, Mosta and Valletta. A café and tourist shop in Bastion Square should cater for your needs, or try the Fontanella at 1 Bastion Street for delicious home-made pastries and coffee served outside at a table on the city walls (see **RESTAURANTS 2**).

The best way of returning to the main gate is to wander at will through the narrow streets, drinking in the unique atmosphere of 'The Silent City' and enjoying the details on the carved doors with their brass knockers, many in the form of diving dolphins, the wrought-iron balconies and street lamps, and the sudden glimpses into delightful little courtyards filled with bougainvillea and geraniums.

Accidents & Breakdowns: If you have a car accident call the police immediately and wait for them to come. On no account move the vehicles, even if you are causing a hold-up, as this will invalidate any insurance claim. In the case of a breakdown call the company from which you hired the vehicle. If you cannot get through to them, there is also a 24-hr breakdown service which can be contacted by calling 829374 (day) or 680502 (night). See **Car Hire**, **Driving**, **Emergency Numbers**, **Police**.

Accommodation: The National Tourism Organization (see **Tourist Information**) produces a comprehensive list of hotels, tourist complexes and guesthouses on the islands. These are classified according to an official rating system, ranging from five-star to one-star accommodation, which is tied to maximum prices that can be charged and facilities provided. The best hotel on Gozo is Ta'Cenc, an old converted manor house renowned for its food.

In addition to hotel rooms, there are many out-of-town flats and villas for rent which can be located either through the nearest tourist office or by looking in the local *Times* (see **Newspapers**). Rates are usually given by the day and are agreed privately.

There are no official camping or caravanning facilities on any of the islands. See **Youth Hostels**.

Air Force Memorial: The War Graves Commission maintains this memorial to the men of the Commonwealth Air Forces who died defending Malta in World War II (see **A-Z**). The pillar engraved with their names is crowned by a globe and gilded eagle, and is surrounded by flower gardens at City Gate, Valletta.

Airport: The airport serving Malta and its neighbouring islands is situated at Luqa, about 6 km south of Valletta. It is fairly small and modern, and offers only rather basic facilities, including a very small takeaway bar and café, and a larger, more expensive, restaurant. There are car-hire operators (see **A-Z**) in the main entrance hall. You can reach town on Bus 36 which stops on the main road outside the airport complex and will take you to the main bus terminal in Valletta. Taxis (see **A-Z**) are parked at the entrance – beware of touts who expect a tip for show-ing you to one.

In addition to the numerous charter flights coming in and out of Malta every day, Air Malta, tel: 824330, and British Airways, tel: 622233, both operate daily scheduled flights to and from Britain (flying time about 3 hr). There are also flights to Malta from all over Europe. For flight information, tel: 623455-8.

Ancient Sites: The Maltese islands have been inhabited for at least 6000 years and the earliest settlers left behind plenty of evidence of their skill in stone cutting and building in the form of temples and hut settlements which can still be seen in a wonderfully preserved condi-tion all over the islands. The flint they used to make their tools was brought over from Sicily, and it may well have been from there that the first Maltese people came. With the introduction of bronze, and later still iron, brought by Phoenician traders, Malta's position at the heart of the civilized world began to have commercial importance. There are

Catacombs, Rabat

signs that the Greeks came to the island, leaving behind coins and arte-facts which can be seen in the National Museum of Archaeology (see **MUSEUMS**), but once the Romans began to dominate the Mediterranean it was only a matter of time before Malta came under their jurisdiction. In 218 BC, the island, with its safe harbours, timber, vineyards and some of the best cotton outside North Africa, became a favoured destination for Roman consuls and offered a good vantage point from which to conduct the wars with Carthage. The remains from this period are rather poor, but a few villas with their mosaics, bathhouses, and advanced plumbing systems can still be seen. The best examples are the villa at Rabat (see **ANCIENT SITES 2**, **EXCURSION 3**) and the baths at Għajn Tuffieħa (see **EXCURSION 2**). See **ANCIENT SITES 1 & 2**.

Architecture: Malta has been invaded many times in its history and buildings erected by one set of rulers have largely been erased by their successors. Although the Arab foundations of some parts of the walls at

Mdina (see **WALK 3**, **A-Z**) can just be seen and some of the old palaces there show Spanish influence dating from the 14thC, it was the Knights of St. John (see **A-Z**) who really left their mark on the island. Coming as they did from all over Europe they left a distinctly European stamp on everything they built: for instance it was an Italian architect, Francesco Laparelli, who was employed to design the defences of Valletta. Gerolamo Cassar (see **A-Z**), the Maltese architect who actually designed most of the city's *auberges* (see **A-Z**), churches and palaces, was also heavily influenced by European models. The results, however, make Valletta one of the major architectural sights of the Mediterranean.

The other main architectural feature of the islands, resulting from the zeal of the Roman Catholic population, is the abundance of massive parish churches dotting the countryside of Malta and Gozo, around which little collections of houses cluster (see **CHURCHES**).

Auberges: Only four of the original *auberges* built in Valletta to house the visiting Knights of St. John (see **A-Z**) during the 16thC look today much as they did then; and the only one of these readily accessible to the public is the Auberge de Provence, now housing the National Museum of Archaeology (see **MUSEUMS**). The others are the Auberge d'Aragon on Independence Square, now the Ministry of Industry; the Auberge de Bavière and the Auberge d'Italie on Merchants Street, now the Main Post Office; and the Auberge de Castille et León (see **WALK 1**), now the Prime Minister's office. The last was completely rebuilt in the 18thC when a much more elaborate facade with shutters and carved stone decorations was added. In Vittoriosa (see **A-Z**) the Auberge

d'Angleterre, Mistral Street; the Auberge de France, Britannic Street (now the Museum of Political History); the less striking Auberge d'Aragon; and the Auberge de Provence et Auvergne next door, have survived out of the town's original seven residences.

Baby-sitters: The larger hotels have a baby-sitter listening service available on request, and some have crèche facilities; otherwise look in the local press (see **Newspapers**) for advertised services. See **Children**.

Banks: See **Currency**, **Money**, **Opening Times**.

Bathing: You can swim off all parts of the coasts of Malta, Gozo and Comino, but there are relatively few sheltered, sandy beaches, and those tend to become rather crowded in summer. Consequently, you may find it more convenient to sunbathe, swim and snorkel (the clear water is excellent for this) from the smooth rocks bordering many of the bays, although this may not be suitable for small children who may also prefer the facilities available at sheltered beaches such as Golden Bay and Mellieña Bay where there are sailboards, pedaloes and surf skis for hire as well as sea-sausage rides, water-skiing and boat trips around the bay.

Of the three islands, Comino in particular has some of the best bathing and diving in the Mediterranean.

See **BEACHES 1 & 2**, **CHILDREN**, **Children**, **Water Sports**.

Best Buys: There is a wide variety of things to buy to remind you of your holiday. Malta's textile industry goes back centuries and today the manufacture of cotton clothing, including jeans and T-shirts, and table and bed linen, is an important source of income. Hand-made lace, often used to trim tablecloths, is another speciality and you may see lacemakers at work in the streets, particularly on Gozo.

Elegant brass dolphin door-knockers are peculiarly Maltese. Some of the best examples can be seen on the ancient carved doors of Mdina (see **WALK 3**) where you will also see them for sale in the shops.

Factories where you can watch glass-blowers at work and buy their wares include Mdina Glass Ltd and Marfa Glass-blowers in the Ta Qali Craft Village (see **ARTS & CRAFTS**), and Phoenician Glass Blowers Ltd on Manoel Island (see **WALK 2**) who offer a free boat ride to their premises from Sliema (0800-1630 Mon.-Fri., 0800-1400 Sat.).

Delicate silver filigree work is another Maltese speciality which can be found both in the craft centres and in specialist silver shops.

Marsaxlokk and Valletta Sunday markets, roadside stalls on Gozo, and small shops everywhere sell reasonably-priced hand-knitted jumpers. Lastly, you will find little *objets d'art* carved from local limestone, *tal-franka*, on Gozo; while on Malta too, the soft stone is sculpted into souvenir statues and ashtrays. See **ARTS & CRAFTS**, **MARKETS**, **SHOPPING 1 & 2**, **Markets**, **Shopping**.

Bicycle & Motorcycle Hire:
Bicycles can be rented by the day
(Lm1) or the week (Lm5) from Fun
Rental Centre, 181 The Strand,
Gzira, and Mosta Cycle Store, 135
Eucharistic Congress Street, Mosta.
To hire a motorcycle you must be
over 18 years of age and hold a
car licence. The cost is Lm3.50 per
day (minimum three days for 80 or
100 cc machines, longer for larger
models) including insurance and
helmet. There is also an 'excess' of
Lm25, this being the amount you
will have to pay before your insurance covers any damage incurred.
Motorcycles can be hired from
Peter's Scooter Shop, 175a rue
d'Argens, and Albert's Scooter
Shop, 216 rue d'Argens, Gzira,
Buġibba; Laronde, Upper Gardens,
St. Julian's; and Victoria Garage,
150 Main Gate Street, Victoria
(Rabat), Gozo (mopeds Lm4 per
day, bicycles Lm1 per day).
As the island roads tend to be narrow and full of potholes, and car
drivers tend to be erratic, take
great care when cycling or driving
a scooter or motorcycle.

Blue Grotto: Bus 32, 33, 34 (or 36 high season only) to Żurrieq, or
Bus 35 to Qrendi then walk. The pounding of the sea has eaten away at
the limestone along this part of the coastline, forming it into caves and
archways, coves and cliffs. The famous Blue Grotto can be viewed
from a point above the village of Wied iż-Żurrieq, but really to see

inside you must enter it by boat. Try and go on a calm, sunny morning when the light will create the best effects in the cave's interior. See **EXCURSION 3**, **Boat Trips**, **Tours**.

Boat Trips: Several companies offer cruises around Grand Harbour and Malta, and to Gozo, Comino, Sicily and Tunisia: Captain Morgan and Jylland boats leave from Sliema Marina; the Gozo Channel Co. Ltd runs ferries from Sa Maison and Ćirkewwa to Mġarr, Gozo; Virtu Rapid Ferries Ltd operates to Tunisia and to Sicily. See **Ferries**.
Of all the boat trips on offer, one which takes you round the harbours of Valletta, so crucial to the history of the island, is undoubtedly the best way of appreciating the great Citadel and its fortifications (see **FORTIFICATIONS**). Also recommended is Captain Morgan's 'Round Malta Day Cruise' which includes a photo-opportunity at the Popeye Village (see **CHILDREN**). Other enjoyable cruises take in the Blue Grotto (see **A-Z**) and St. Paul's Island (see **A-Z**). See **Water-taxis**.

British Connection: Admiral Nelson successfully blockaded Grand Harbour (see **FORTIFICATIONS**) with the help of the Portuguese and, in 1799, set up a provisional administration. The Treaty of Paris, which brought the islands officially into the British Empire as a Crown Colony, was signed in 1814. Thereafter much was done to extend the facilities of Grand Harbour and the fortifications of the island generally, as the British again recognized the island's strategic importance, particularly during the Crimean War. Many Maltese fought for the British during World War I, but political unease was developing, and in 1921 self-government was granted. The situation became unstable however, and this constitution was revoked in 1936, returning the island to Crown Colony status. World War II (see **A-Z**) again saw the Maltese fighting bravely on the side of the British in the face of sustained Italian and German attack, and much assistance was given by Britain to aid the island's recovery afterwards. Malta continued to be a major British RN and RAF base throughout the 1950s, but, following a national referendum, independence was granted in 1964 (although a British military presence continued until 1979). In 1989 Malta celebrated 25 years of freedom – the first period of self-rule since before the birth of Christ!

Budget:

Hotel breakfast	Lm1.50
Lunch	from Lm2.65
Snack (pizza)	Lm1-1.50
Dish of the Day	Lm2
Cinema ticket	Lm2
Museum ticket	15c
Tea	20c
Coffee	25c
House wine	from Lm1.50 (per bottle)
Beer	25c
Bus ticket	12c (for 10-min journey)

Buses: All Maltese buses begin and end their journeys at the City Gate terminus beside the Triton Fountain (see **A–Z**) in Valletta. A board at the terminus displays bus numbers, destinations and departure times; and a map containing the same information is available from tourist offices (see **Tourist Information**).

Buses are frequent, often extremely crowded and very cheap (Sliema to Valletta costs around 12c). They run until 2300 in towns, and until 2130 to outlying areas. Pay the driver as you enter.

Gozo buses run less frequently but it is still possible to reach most villages on the daily service into and out of Victoria (Rabat). The bus terminus is located just off Republic Street on Main Gate Street in Victoria. See **Transport**.

Cameras & Photography: The usual brands of internationally-known film are widely available. It is also easy to find places offering same-day developing for prints; however, slides generally take about ten days. There are good photographic shops in Valletta and Sliema where you can purchase cameras and accessories (see **SHOPPING 1 & 2**). Photography is prohibited in some churches and museums and in the Manoel Theatre (see **Theatre**), so check before you snap! Remember, too, to ask permission before you photograph local people, however used they appear to be to tourists, as it is possible they may take offence.

Car Hire: There are plenty of local car-hire firms in Malta to choose from, but be warned, the standard of some of the vehicles they rent out leaves a lot to be desired. In view of this you may want to hire from one of the international firms. Avis has offices at the airport (see **A–Z**) and at 50 Msida Seafront (head office), and branches at the Hilton Hotel, St. Julian's; the Corinthia Palace Hotel, Attard; the Jerma Palace Hotel, Marsaskala; and in Mistra Village, St. Paul's Bay. Hertz can be found at United Garage Ltd, 66 St. Paul's Bay and United Garage Ltd, 66 Gzira Road, Gzira. One of the best local car-hire fleets is run by Wembleys at 50 St. George's Road, St. Julian's (head office) and Rental Station, St. Andrew's Road, St. Andrew's.

Car-hire companies on Gozo include Victor J. Borg Enterprises, Gozo Garage, 5 Xagħra Road, Victoria, and Mayo Rent-a-Car and Pardi Motors, New Building, Republic Street, Victoria.

To hire a car you must be over 21 years of age (for Hertz) and hold a valid UK licence and passport. Prices range from Lm7 per day for a Ford Fiesta to Lm11 for jeeps and minibuses. Check that the rate you are quoted includes insurance. See **Accidents & Breakdowns**, **Driving**.

Cassar, Gerolamo (d. 1586): The Maltese architect and engineer in charge of the layout and building of Valletta, which is a tribute to his simple, functional but pleasing designs. He was responsible for all the *auberges* (see **A-Z**) and many of the city's churches, but his greatest contribution was probably St. John's Co-Cathedral & Oratory (see **CHURCHES, A-Z**) which was unfinished on his death in 1586. His work was carried on by his son, Vittorio. See **Architecture**, **Grand Master's Palace & Armoury**.

Cathedral & Museum, Gozo: The Cathedral at Victoria (Rabat) was built between 1697 and 1711 to the design of Lorenzo Gafa. It is a relatively simple Roman baroque building without the usual dome, but when you get inside and look up, the effect of a dome has been created by a remarkable painting on the ceiling. The Museum is situated at the back of the Cathedral and contains the Church of the Assumption's treasures, including silver and gold ceremonial items, paintings, religious archives and sacred vestments. It is open 1100-1600 Mon.-Sat. (closed hol.) and costs 15c (children under ten, free).

Chemists: A roster of late-night and Sunday-opening chemists is posted in the Sunday local paper, *The* (Maltese) *Sunday Times* (see **Newspapers**). Chemimart, part of the Boots chain, has branches at 3 Misrah il-Helsien, Valletta and 14 St. Anne Square, Floriana. See **Health.**

Children: The Maltese islanders, like Italians, dote on children and make them welcome in restaurants and in bars (there are no restrictions). Entertaining children is relatively easy here as you can always take them swimming or to one of the many public playgrounds which exist in most towns and villages (e.g. in front of the Hilton Hotel, St. Julian's; on the Gzira waterfront; outside the main gate to Mdina; and in the middle of Mosta behind the church). These are well-equipped with slides, roundabouts, seesaws, swings, etc. (0700-1900). For a special treat, there are also the internationally-renowned Italian circuses, such as Cesare Togni, that regularly visit the island, putting on several shows a day (up to Lm5 for adults, Lm2.50 for children, free for the

handicapped). There are several possible sites such as the St. Andrew's Ground at Ta Qali and on Manoel Island, so ask for further details at the tourist office (see **Tourist Information**) and look out for posters. See CHILDREN, **Baby-sitters**, **Bathing**.

Cinemas: Up-to-date, English-language films are shown at the Ambassador, the Embassy, the Gawhra and the Gojjell in Valletta, and the Alhambra in Sliema. The University of Malta (see **A-Z**) also has a film club which shows interesting films weekly in the Assembly Hall. Gozo has three cinemas, all in Victoria (Rabat). Check local press for current programmes. See **Newspapers**, **What's On**.

Climate: The winter months, between November and April, are the coolest and wettest. Summer can be very hot, especially in July and August, making May-June and September-October perhaps the most pleasant months in which to visit. There are several local winds which blow up unpredictably, including the autumn *gregale*, a cold north-westerly wind which only blows for two or three days at a time, and the hot sirocco from the south which carries sand from the Sahara.

Comino: Comino is a tiny island farmed by a small community. It is named Kemmuna in Maltese, after the spice, cumin, which grows wild here among the rocks. There are no cars on the island, which is criss-crossed with little footpaths making it easy to walk around the coast or cut back at any point to the central 'road' running from the 17thC tower (built by Grand Master Aloph de Wignacourt to defend the Gozo channel), past the remains of the Knights' isolation hospital and the island's chapel, to Santa Marija Bay and the Club Nautico. The waters around the island are supposed to be the least polluted in the whole of the Mediterranean and therefore *the* place to snorkel, dive and swim (look out for sunken treasure – the Blue Lagoon was once a pirates' haven). The hire of watersports equipment can be arranged at the hotel if you book at least a day in advance (inc. use of private beach at San Niklaw Bay). See BEACHES 2, **Boat Trips**, **Ferries**.

Complaints: Ask to see the manager if you have a problem, or contact the National Tourist Organization (see **Tourist Information**).

Consulates:
UK – 7 St. Anne's Street, Floriana, tel: 233134-8.
Australia – Airways House, Gaiety Lane, Sliema, tel: 338201-5.
USA – Development House, St. Anne's Street, Floriana, tel: 623653/620424/623216.

Conversion Chart:

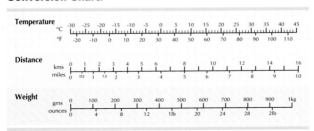

Cospicua (Bormla): Bus 1, 2, 4, 6. Cospicua, one of the so-called 'three cities' which predate Valletta, is sandwiched between the outer walls of Senglea (see **A–Z**), another of the 'three cities', the earliest of the outer walls built in the whole area, and the massive bastions of the Cotonera Lines (see **FORTIFICATIONS**). The town was badly damaged in World War II. See **FESTIVALS**.

Credit Cards: See **Money**.

Crime & Theft: Malta is a small island and crime is not a major problem, although there have been some reports of bag snatching in town. Nevertheless, take the usual precautions and keep all valuables and large amounts of cash in the hotel safe. Report any theft immediately to the police. See **Consulates**, **Emergency Numbers**, **Insurance**, **Police**.

Currency: The Maltese pound, known locally as lira (Lm), is divided into one hundred cents (c). Notes are in denominations of Lm2, 5, 10 and 20. Coins in circulation are worth Lm1 and 1c, 2c, 5c, 10c, 25c and 50c. A cent is made up of ten mils (m), but these are worth so little you may only rarely come across the scarce 2m, 3m and 5m coins in your change. The Central Bank of Malta also issues gold and silver coins of special interest to collectors, which are legal tender. See **Money**.

Customs: Cover arms and legs when visiting churches or you may be refused entry. Topless bathing is on the increase, but only well away from towns – the Maltese islanders are still quite strict in this respect, despite the influx of tourists and the influence of film and television, so try not to offend local sensibilities.
It is a long-standing tradition to take a family walk, known as the *passeggiata*, in the late afternoon/early evening. On Sundays this is preferably done out of town, Marsaxlokk, St. Paul's Bay and Buġibba being favourite destinations (you will find their streets clogged with cars at this time). If people-watching is a hobby of yours, have a drink at a waterside bar or café and enjoy the weekly parade of Maltese life:

young parents proudly pushing prams followed by gloating grannies, and engaged couples shyly holding hands in the company of watchful elders.

Customs Allowances:

Duty Free Into:	Cigarettes	or	Cigars	or	Tobacco		Spirits	or	Wine
Malta	300		75		400 g		1.5 *l*		2 *l*
UK	200		50		250 g		1*l*		2 *l*

Dentists: See **Health**.

Dgħajjes: See **Water-taxis**.

Dingli Cliffs: Bus 81. These limestone cliffs along part of Malta's southwestern coast are quite spectacular and definitely well worth visiting. A road runs along the clifftop, but you will find it more rewarding to explore the area's old chapels and prehistoric monuments on foot. See **EXCURSION 3**.

Disabled Travellers: There have been real attempts by the Maltese government to provide for the disabled, particularly for anyone confined to a wheelchair; for example, some parks have been equipped with ramps and there are special parking facilities in Palace Square, Valletta. Nevertheless, there are still major difficulties because of the height of the kerbstones and the generally poor condition of pavement and road surfaces. Hotels purporting to offer facilities for the disabled were found in fact to be deficient, in that doorways were often rather too narrow and lifts inadequate. The National Tourism Organization (see **Tourist Information**) will provide you with a coded list of hotels offering special facilities. See **Parking**.

Drinks: Local beer is both excellent and cheap; bottled and draught Hop Leaf pale ale and Cisk lager are available everywhere. In contrast, locally-made wines won't win any international awards, although the better ones are drinkable and improving. There are two grades, distinguishable by their prices: rough house wines costing up to 40c a bottle, and better table wines at around 75-90c. Marsovin Special Reserve (red and white) is good value, as is Lachryma Vitis Green Label. Marsovin Palazzo Verdala is a particularly clean white wine, and there are some pleasant rosés as well. If you can track down local wine actually made on Gozo from grapes grown on the island, you will find it a strong and flavourful drink, quite unlike its factory-made cousins from Malta. Imported wines and beers are also usually available, but cost more. Most of Malta's tap water comes from wells and desalination plants – and tastes like it! It is safe to drink, but unpleasant, so you will probably prefer to buy bottled water for drinking. Imported mineral water is more expensive so if you buy a local brand, check that it is spring water. The usual range of internationally-known soft drinks is widely available.

Driving: Malta has inherited the British habit of driving on the left so all island cars have right-hand drive. Most of the same traffic rules also apply here, except at roundabouts where traffic joining has priority (leading to much confusion). Road surfaces, lighting and signposting are poor, and white lines practically non-existent, so take particular care at night. There is a speed restriction of 65 kph out of town and 40 kph in built-up areas. Local driving tends, on the whole, to be inconsiderate and local vehicles dilapidated, so take care. See **Accidents & Breakdowns**, **Car Hire**, **Parking**, **Petrol**.

Drugs: All drugs are illegal and there are severe penalties for offenders. There is a Detox Centre at St. Luke's Hospital (see **Health**).

Dwejra: Bus 5. The sea has broken through the cliffs on this part of Gozo's western coastline below San Lawrenz, widening out into a sheltered, crystal-clear pool known as Il-Qawra. Fungus Rock, which is named after a plant once collected by the Knights of St. John (see **A-Z**), stands just off the shore; and It-Tieqa, a huge natural stone arch, forms a perfect natural frame through which to view the sea as it pounds against the massive limestone cliffs. See **EXCURSION 4**.

Eating Out: There are lots of possibilities for eating out in Malta – ranging from roadside bakeries to bistros and elegant restaurants serving international cuisine. Resort towns, such as Buġibba, contain numerous touristy cafés serving chips with everything, but there are also good-value Italian and Chinese establishments to be found if you take the trouble to look around. Some restaurants offer a reasonably-priced tourist menu, including a starter, main course and dessert, for about Lm2.50. A full meal with wine and coffee at a smart restaurant will cost somewhere in the region of Lm12 for two – not expensive by European standards. Places serving genuine Maltese dishes are a little more difficult to track down, but are worth the effort. See **RESTAURANTS 1 & 2**, **Food**.

Electricity: 240V, single phase, 50 cycles. British square three-pin plugs are used.

Emergency Numbers:

Police:	Malta 191
	Gozo 556011
Fire:	Malta 199
	Gozo 55
Ambulance:	Malta 196
	Gozo 96

Events:

31 March: Freedom Day, celebrating the closure of the last British base on the island in 1979; a military parade before the President and Prime Minister, wreath-laying at one of the island's war memorials and an event such as a boat race in the afternoon.

Last week April-first week May: Folk Festival; groups all over the islands sing, dance and play traditional music. Dates, venues and artists vary – check with tourist office (see **Tourist Information**).

1 May: Worker's Day, instituted by the Labour government under the auspices of the Feast of St. Joseph the Worker; traditional May Day parades with a political flavour.

End June: Mnarja Festival, Buskett Gardens (Bus 81), originally associated with the bringing in of the harvest; feasting (traditionally on rabbit), singing and dancing the evening before the festival, and displays of farm produce and bare-back horse and donkey racing in the afternoon. See PARKS & GARDENS.

21 September: Independence Day, celebrating independence from Britain in 1964; events and locations vary from year to year – check with tourist office (see **Tourist Information**).

13 December: Republic Day; bands, parades, speeches and fireworks celebrating the founding of the Republic State of Malta in 1974. See FESTIVALS, **Newspapers**, **What's On**.

Ferries: You can reach Mgarr on the south coast of Gozo (see **A-Z**) on one of the car and passenger ferries which Gozo Channel Co. Ltd runs from Cirkewwa on the north coast of Malta (30 min) and from Sa Maison, Pietà Creek, near Valletta (1 hr 15 min). There are also boats leaving the Customs Quay, Grand Harbour at noon on weekdays (1 hr

30 min), and a hydrofoil. Full timetables are available from tourist offices (see **Tourist Information**) and are published in *The Times* (see **Newspapers**) and *What's On* guide (see **What's On**).

The Gozo Channel Co. Ltd runs a launch daily to Comino (see **A-Z**) from Ċirkewwa, Malta and from Mġarr, Gozo (April-Oct.). For further details, contact the company at Hay Wharf, Sa Maison, tel: 603964/5; Ċirkewwa, tel: 471884; and Mġarr, Gozo, tel: 556016. During the summer the Comino Hotel also runs a ferry service from Ċirkewwa departing at 0730, 0935, 1140, 1530 and 1725; return trips at 0650, 0905, 1110, 1450 and 1645. See **Boat Trips**.

Filfla: This island off the southwest coast of Malta has been declared a nature reserve and visitors are not permitted to land.

Floriana: The suburb of Floriana, a short walk from the bus terminus at Valletta, lies between City Gate and the outer defensive walls of the city. One of the first features you see as you walk towards the Church of St. Publius from the terminus is a paved area, now used as a car park, which is covered in strange round stumps which look like the remains of huge columns. They are in fact the lids of enormous underground granaries built by the Knights of St. John (see **A-Z**) to withstand a further siege. At the end of The Mall you will find the Argotti Botanic Gardens (see **PARKS & GARDENS**) and the circular Sarria Chapel with its silver dome. You can see for miles across the sprawl of Valletta's suburbs from the walls. See **WALK 2**.

Food: It is not always easy to find restaurants specializing in Maltese dishes as, especially in resorts, the usual international cuisine or fast food predominates. However, it is worth the effort of finding somewhere where you can sample local dishes, many of which feature delicious freshly-caught fish.

Bragioli – beef wrapped around a stuffing with olives.
Ross il-Forn – savoury rice dish baked with eggs and meat.
Fenek – rabbit often casseroled with wine.
Espadon, pesce spada – swordfish.
Acciola – amberjack.

Hobz bizet – snack consisting of a roll filled with tuna, olives, tomato, lettuce and onion.
See **RESTAURANTS 1 & 2**, **Eating Out**.

Ghadira Nature Reserve: This small area, just below the bus terminus and behind the beach at Mellieħa, is a designated nature reserve which has recently won a diploma of merit from *Europa Nostra*. It is not yet open to the public, although party visits can be arranged in advance by contacting the Ornithological Society, PO Box 498, Valletta. With good binoculars you might be able to see some of the larger birds that come to the pools here. See **BEACHES 1**, **EXCURSION 2**.

Gozo: The atmosphere on this island is quite different to that of Malta. It is still a relative backwater with quiet, rural communities living in isolated villages separated by open rolling countryside and surviving by subsistence farming and fishing. Nevertheless, the tourist industry is beginning to make an impact, and the villages of Xlendi and Marsalforn in particular, while still pretty and atmospheric, are besieged by day-trippers from Malta.

The major sights of the island include Xewkija, Ta'Pinu (see **CHURCHES**), Ggantija (see **ANCIENT SITES 1**), the beaches at Marsalforn, Xlendi and Ramla Bay (see **BEACHES 2**), and the capital, Victoria (Rabat), with its Citadel (see **FORTIFICATIONS**). The windmill at Qala is reputedly the last one still in use on the islands; and the Knights' washhouse, on the Xlendi road out of Victoria (Rabat), built beside a gushing spring, Għajn il-Kbira, is now used by the local women to do their weekly clothes wash. See **EXCURSION 4**, **Boat Trips**, **Ferries**, **Tours**.

Grand Master's Palace & Armoury:
Designed and built by Gerolamo Cassar (see **A–Z**) around a house originally constructed in 1569, the palace is centred around two courtyards and consists of unostentatious living quarters and grand state apartments, as well as the Armoury which is said to hold one of the finest collections of weaponry in Europe and includes a suit of armour decorated with gold dating from the early 1600s. The island's parliament meets in the Council Chamber surrounded by beautiful Gobelin tapestries; the Hall of St. Michael and St. George is painted with scenes of the Great Siege (see **A–Z**) and on one wall is a remarkable balcony made from the remains of the ship in which the Knights of St. John (see **A–Z**) made their escape from Rhodes. See **BUILDINGS, SQUARES, World War II**.

BUCKINGHAM PALACE

THE GOVERNOR,
MALTA.

TO HONOUR HER BRAVE PEOPLE
I AWARD THE GEORGE CROSS
TO THE ISLAND FORTRESS OF MALTA
TO BEAR WITNESS TO A HEROISM AND
DEVOTION THAT WILL LONG BE FAMOUS
IN HISTORY.

GEORGE R.I.

APRIL 15TH 1942.

Great Siege: When the Knights of St. John (see **A–Z**) first came to Malta they knew that it was only a matter of time before Suleiman the Magnificent, Sultan of the Ottoman Empire, once again gathered his forces against this outpost of militant Christianity. In fact it was 35 years before the attack came, a period during which the Knights fortified the little town of Birgu (now Vittoriosa – see **A–Z**) with the great fort of St. Angelo, and protected the harbour with Fort St. Elmo, and Senglea with Fort St. Michael. In April 1565 Grand Master La Valette got word that a huge army, led by Mustapha Pasha, had left Constantinople in hundreds of ships under the command of Admiral Piali. La Valette was prepared, the storehouses were full, his men were well trained and supervised, but he knew he was outnumbered by a ratio of something like four to one.

The Turks tried to take Fort St. Elmo first, believing the poorly-sited bastion would fall within days. They were wrong; the Knights held out for over a month and the Turks lost some 8000 men. They next tried their

Fort St. Angelo

strength against Fort St. Angelo. Meanwhile, however, a small number of Christian soldiers managed to land at Kalkara (see **A-Z**) after crossing from Sicily, greatly boosting the morale of the besieged Knights. In early July the attack started on the forts of St. Angelo and St. Michael and continued mercilessly through August. The Knights and their men were on their last legs when rumours reached them that a relief force was on its way from Sicily. The Turks too, had suffered massive losses and when they heard that Christian reinforcements were on their way from where they had landed, decided to withdraw. The Great Siege was at last over after four months and the deaths of around 30,000 Turks, 250 Knights and 15,000 Christian soldiers. See **FORTIFICATIONS**, **Sciortino**.

Guides: See **Tourist Information**.

Hairdressers: The Dragonara Palace Hotel, the Hilton International and the Holiday Inn all have up-market salons. Local hairdressers do a good job, as long as you don't want anything too exotic, and their prices are much more reasonable.

Health: British holiday-makers staying on Malta for less than a month are eligible for free medical treatment. Doctors can be seen at one of the seven local 24-hr polyclinics at Floriana, tel: 603314; Gzira, tel: 514085; Cospicua, tel: 775492; Mosta, tel: 496563; Rabat, tel: 649002; and Paola, tel: 622103; and on Gozo, tel: 556851. The main hospital on Malta is St. Luke's, Gwardamanga, tel: 621251/607860, and on Gozo, Gozo General Hospital, tel: 556851. You will find that just about everyone speaks English.

Dental surgeries, operating on individual timetables, are also held at the above polyclinics. In addition, Dr H. Messina Ferrante, 292/8 Republic Street, Valletta, tel: 226483/626483, provides private emergency dental treatment.

Local hazards to watch out for include heatstroke and sunburn in the middle of summer, and the sea urchins on some rocky shores. If you are prone to upset stomach from dietary changes, bring a reliable drug with you and consult a doctor if symptoms persist. See **Chemists, Emergency Numbers, Insurance.**

Howard Gardens: These gardens in front of the main gate to Mdina are well planted with palms and flowerbeds and contain a children's playground, clean toilets, plenty of shady seats, a *karrozzin* stand (see **A-Z**) and a nearby café – a good spot to relax after a stroll round 'The Silent City'. See **EXCURSION 3, WALK 3.**

Inquisitor's Summer Palace: A summerhouse from the days of the Knights' (see **A-Z**) overlordship of the island, built in 1625 by Inquisitor Honoratus Visconti. Inquisitors were invited to Malta as representatives of the Pope, but their methods of torture, their arrogance, power and privilege led to them being reviled by the Knights and the islanders alike. The palace is surprisingly beautiful, standing as it does near the dramatic southwest coast. See **EXCURSION 3.**

Insurance: You should take out adequate travel insurance before you leave home, covering you against theft and loss of property and money, as well as medical expenses (in case of repatriation) for the duration of your stay. Your travel agent or bank should be able to recommend a suitable policy. See **Crime & Theft**, **Driving**, **Health.**

Kalkara: Bus 4. Kalkara occupies the headland which juts out into Grand Harbour between Fort St. Angelo and Fort Ricasoli, and is bounded by Kalkara Creek and Rinella Bay. It was in Kalkara Creek that the 'Little Relief' of Christian reinforcements led by Chevalier de Robles landed to reach the beleaguered Knights during the Great Siege of 1565 (see **A–Z**). The largest building here today is the huge ex-Royal Naval Hospital.

Karm, Dun (1871-1961): Malta's national poet whose major claim to fame is that he wrote the words for the island's National Anthem. See **BUILDINGS**.

Karrozzini: *Karrozzini* are horse-drawn cabs which can be hired for a relaxing sightseeing trip round town. Arrange a price and a route before you set off. In Valletta you will find them in Great Siege Square, at City Gate by the bus terminus, and outside the Lower Barracca Gardens (see **PARKS & GARDENS**). There is also a stand outside Mdina Gate, Mdina (see **A–Z**). See **Transport**.

Kennedy Memorial: Bus 43, 44, 45, 49 to Salina Bay. This elegant stone memorial stands next to the sea in a pine grove at the head of Salina Bay, on the right of the road to St. Paul's Bay. It is a favourite Sunday picnic spot for many Maltese people. There is a playground for children. See **EXCURSION 2.**

Knights' Armoury, Gozo: This building in the Citadel at Victoria (Rabat) (see **FORTIFICATIONS**) was restored by the Knights (see **A-Z**) in 1776 to house their armour and weaponry. It was used by the British as a headquarters during World War II (see **A-Z**). To reach the Armoury turn left off the Cathedral Square as you face the church. It is open 0845-1515 (closed hol.) and costs 15c.

Knights of St. John: The Knights of the Sovereign Military Hospitaller Order of St. John of Jerusalem, of Rhodes and of Malta first came to Malta in November 1530 after months of fighting the Turks, who had driven them from their previous stronghold on Rhodes, where they had been based for over 200 years, in 1522.

The Order was founded on the pilgrim route to Jerusalem around the year 1000 and was dedicated to taking in exhausted travellers, looking after the sick, and protecting pilgrims from attack along the way. As the Crusades got under way the Knights attracted recruits from the noblest families of Europe, greatly increasing the Order's status and leading to the accumulation of vast wealth. Gradually it became more militant in heading the Christian fight against Islam.

Malta at this time was under the sway of the Spanish and, after delicate negotiation, it was agreed that the Knights could settle here and pay rent in the form of one falcon a year. Within 35 years the Order was again under attack from the Turks, but finally defeated the enemy after the Great Siege (see **A-Z**) of 1565. The lessons learned from this close-ly-fought contest led them to turn the island into an impregnable fortress (see **FORTIFICATIONS**).

The Knights' rule came to an inglorious end in 1798 when Grand Master Ferdinand von Hompesch signed an armistice with Napoleon after years of easy living and the loss of much of their wealth and membership with the coming of the French Revolution. The Order still exists today (its headquarters are in Rome), providing medical assistance wherever it is needed throughout the world.

Language: Practically everyone on Malta speaks very good English as it is a compulsory school subject, but should you ask for directions in an out-of-the-way corner of Malta or Gozo, you may still find only

Maltese spoken. This obscure and difficult language is interspersed with Arabic, Italian and Spanish words and sounds, and although it is written in the Roman alphabet has several accents modifying the pronunciation. Any attempt to use some simple words such as 'good morning' – *bongu* (with a soft g), 'good night' – *bonswa*, 'thank you' – *grazzi*, 'cheers!' – in English when you are drinking and *ciao* or *sahha* when you are leaving, will delight your hosts.

Laundries: The larger hotels and holiday complexes have their own laundry facilities, and there are self-service launderettes in bigger towns. Square Deal, tel: 220800, and Phoenicia, Great Siege Road, Floriana, tel: 234418/627141 (24-hr answering service), offer a collection and delivery and mending service.

Lost Property: Contact Police Headquarters at Floriana (see **Police**). See **Insurance**.

Markets: Most towns and villages have small general markets one morning a week – for example there is one behind the church in Mosta on Mondays (0800-1230), another (at the same time) in Vittoriosa (see **A-Z**) on Tuesdays, and a third by the Sacred Heart Church in Sliema on Wednesdays. One of the best places to buy fresh produce is at one of the mobile stalls which come in from the countryside. If you are lucky, you might even come across a van with a portable bakery in the back. On Gozo you will also find roadside tables from which sweaters and lacework are sold. See **MARKETS**, **Best Buys**, **Shopping**.

Mdina: Bus 80. Mdina was the earliest capital of Malta and excavations have shown that there were people here long before the Romans came. The Romans had their capital here although there is some dispute as to whether the governor, St. Publius, had his house here. The period of Arab rule saw the first fortifications being built here and since then each successive occupying nation has left its mark on the architecture (see **A-Z**). One of the common names for the Citadel is 'The Silent City' and a stroll around its narrow streets or a ride in a horse-drawn *karrozzin* (see **A-Z**) will give you a sense of the long history of the island. Look out in particular for the Vilhena Palace, now the Museum of Natural History (see **MUSEUMS**), which stands on your right as you enter Mdina Gate, and Palazzo Falzon, often known as the Norman House (see **BUILDINGS**), which is located in Villegaignon Street. See **EXCURSION 3**, **WALK 3**.

Mediterranean Congress Centre: The Hospital of the Order of the Knights of St. John (see **A-Z**) in Valletta was converted in 1979, and the main exhibition centre is in what was formerly the Sacra Infermeria. There is also a plush restaurant beneath the vaulted ceiling of the Soldiers' Ward.

Between meetings the main conference hall is used to stage theatrical productions. However, the centre suffered a fire in 1987 and this area is currently undergoing reconstruction. The Malta Experience, a 'multivision show', gives visitors a visual and musical tour through Malta's history and culture. See **BUILDINGS**, **WALK 1**.

Money: The main banks with branches throughout the islands are the Bank of Valletta and the Mid-Med Bank. Bureaux de change are open outside normal opening times (see **A-Z**). To obtain the latest foreign exchange-rate information offered on the Mid-Med Bank's Dial-A-Rate 24-hr service, tel: 495478. All the well-known traveller's cheques are acceptable on Malta, as are Eurocheques.

Credit cards such as Visa (Barclaycard), Access (Mastercharge and Eurocard), American Express and Diners' Club are widely accepted in hotels, restaurants, shops and businesses catering for tourists. Small car-hire firms, petrol stations, local restaurants and local tour operators, however, may not take them in payment. See **Currency**.

Mosque: Bus 5 to Paola. The green-tiled dome of the mosque with its gilded minaret is hidden away in industrial Paola beside a centre for visiting Libyans. The congregation only amounts, on average, to some 70 Muslim devotees, but the building, which was erected in 1979, testifies to the close ties established between the Maltese and Libyan people during the time of the Labour government which ended in 1987. See **EXCURSION 1**.

Museum of Religious Art: This museum next to Our Lady of Grace Parish Church in Zabbar contains a large collection of religious paintings by unknown Maltese and European artists, many dating from the 15thC and allegedly donated by the Knights of St. John (see **A-Z**). It is open 0930-1200 Sat. & Sun., or by arrangement with Mr Schembri, tel: 827275. Admission is free, but donations are welcome.

Music: You may come across the indigenous music and dance of Malta and Gozo in the form of specially staged tourist entertainments. Like the Maltese language and other aspects of the culture, these have been subject to a mixture of outside influences, and you will see and hear Sicilian and Arab elements both in the music and in the costume.

Classical music events are frequently held in St. John's Co-Cathedral (see **CHURCHES**, **A-Z**) and other large churches around the islands. The palace grounds of the San Anton Gardens, Attard (see **PARKS & GARDENS**) are occasionally the lovely setting for summertime concerts and theatrical productions; and the Buskett Gardens near Rabat (see **PARKS & GARDENS**) are the scene of the annual Mnarja Folk Festival (see **Events**) and other musical events throughout the summer season. See **NIGHTLIFE**, **Nightlife**, **Theatre**.

National Museum of Fine Arts: This collection of historical paintings and sculpture, housed in a lovely old palace on South Street in Valletta, includes a Tintoretto and works from the 14thC to the present day, including some by Maltese artists. Contemporary exhibitions of local artists' works are held in the Loggia. It is open 0745-1345 mid June-Sep.; 0815-1630 Mon.-Sat., 0815-1545 Sun. (Oct.-mid June); closed hol. Entrance is 15c, child 7.5c.

Natural History Museum, Gozo: Gozo's Natural History Museum, situated in the Citadel (see **FORTIFICATIONS**) at Victoria (Rabat), contains displays on the island's geological features, stuffed extinct birds, and fish which still inhabit the surrounding waters. Open 0845-1515, closed hol.; entrance 15c.

New Gallery of the Auberge de Provence: A chance to see inside one of the few *auberges* (see **A-Z**) open to the public. Temporary exhibitions of the work of local painters are held in this gallery inside the National Museum of Archaeology (see **MUSEUMS**). It is open 0745-1345 mid June-Sep.; 0815-1645 Mon.-Sat., 0815-1600 Sun. (Oct.-mid June); closed hol. Entrance is 15c, child 7.5c.

Newspapers: Local English-language papers include *The Times* (of Malta), published daily, and three weeklies: *The Democrat, The Weekend Chronicle* and *The* (Maltese) *Sunday Times.* All have local and international news, and listings. British newspapers are sold on the afternoon of the day of publication. See **Accommodation**, **What's On**.

Nightlife: Valletta is not the place to go looking for wild nightlife; the city is Malta's working capital, not its fun capital. You might find the occasional bar open after 1900 but that's all.
Today it is St. Julian's, Paceville and Sliema which have the casino, the discos and the late-night bars. Most of the large hotels put on their own extensive programmes of in-house entertainment, including singers, comedians, magic shows, cabarets, etc., and most are open to non-residents. The Tignè Court Hotel in Sliema, for instance, holds a regular Poolside Disco Splash Bar-B-Que with a folk-dancing display (Lm5, child Lm3.50), while if you are staying around the St. Paul's Bay area there is a disco at the Black Rose, Islets Promenade, Qawra (part of the New Dolmen Hotel complex near Buġibba). It is also possible to sign up for outside tourist entertainments such as the Farmhouse Night,

involving a visit to a barn set out with trestle tables laden with local specialities (see **Food**) and after-dinner entertainment by folk dancers in traditional costume (Lm5, child Lm3.50).

On Gozo there is a disco which is held in a cave – La Grotta Disco-Night Club, Xlendi Road, Victoria (Rabat) – and hotels, including the Cornucopia in Xagħra, the Calypso in Marsalforn and the Ta'Cenc in Sannat, offer discos, barbecues and live music. Marsalforn is unique in that it can also boast two wine bars: Marlena D in Marina Street and Pink Panther on Xagħra Road, both of which are open from 1830 daily and serve snacks and cocktails. See NIGHTLIFE, RESTAURANTS 1 & 2, **Music, Theatre**.

Opening Times:

Museums, prehistoric sites, galleries – 0745-1400 mid June-Sep.; 0815-1700 Mon.-Sat., 0815-1615 Sun. (Oct.-mid June); closed hol.
Shops – 0900-1230, 1600-1900 Mon.-Fri., 0900-1230 Sat., closed hol.
Banks – 0800-1200 Mon.-Thu., 0800-1200 and 1430-1600 Fri., 0800-1130 Sat. (mid June-Sep.); 0830-1230 Mon.-Thu., 0830-1230 and 1630-1800 Fri., 0830-1200 Sat. (Oct.-mid June); closed hol.
Bars/cafés – 0900-0100.
Main post office – 0730-1800 Mon.-Sat. (mid June-Sep.), 0800-1830 Mon.-Sat (Oct.-mid June).
Post office branches – 0730-1245 Mon.-Sat.
Sub-post offices – 0800-1300, 1600-1800 Mon.-Fri., 0800-1300 Sat.

Orientation: Malta is only about 17.5 miles long by some 8.25 miles wide; and with a population of around 350,000 (plus a tourist influx of 750,000 a year), it is one of the most densely populated places on the face of the earth! Most people live in and around the capital, Valletta, and the towns which now make up its suburbs have almost joined up, giving this part of the island the impression of a building site! However, the advantage of Malta's small size is the speed with which one can escape to its more beautiful spots. The main tourist resorts of Sliema, St. Julian's, Buġibba, St. Paul's Bay and Mellieħa Bay (see BEACHES 1, EXCURSION 2) are on the northeast coast where the land slopes gently to the sea. In contrast, the southwest coast drops dramatically into the sea

South Coast

from great cliffs. Ridges running across the island have been used as defences for centuries and the fortress town of Mdina (see **WALK 3**, **A-Z**), like Victoria (Rabat) on Gozo, stands high on a bluff in the centre of the island.

Gozo (see **A-Z**) and Comino (see **A-Z**) both have the virtue of being small and relatively inaccessible so, with their populations declining through emigration, the pressure on space is nowhere near so intense as on Malta. To avoid confusion between Rabat on Gozo and Rabat on Malta, the former is always referred to as Victoria (Rabat).

It is essential to equip yourself with a good map of the islands before you go; the 1:25,000 map published by the Director of Military Survey (available from Stanfords, 12-14 Longacre, London WC2E 9LP) is excellent, but unavailable on Malta.

Parking: Parking areas are provided at all the major attractions and there are no official charges. Attendants require a contribution (about 20c) when you leave but this is not a set fee. It is inadvisable to take a car into Valletta, but if you do there are parking areas in Palace Square. Parking spaces for disabled drivers are designated. See **Driving**.

Passports & Customs: A valid passport is necessary for entry to Malta, but no visa is required for visits of up to three months. See **Customs Allowances**.

Petrol: Petrol stations close at 1900 (1800 in winter) and do not open at all on Sundays or public holidays, so make sure that you have filled your tank on a Saturday afternoon (long queues build up after 1700). See **Driving**.

Police: Police Headquarters on Malta are in Floriana, tel: 224001, and on Gozo at 113 Republic Street, Victoria (Rabat), tel: 556430/ 556011. There are also police stations in all villages and towns. Police wear a black uniform in winter and khaki in summer (with American-style sunglasses), and are unarmed. Officers are very approachable and all speak good English. See **Accidents & Breakdowns**, **Crime & Theft**, **Emergency Numbers**.

Post Offices: The main post office in Valletta is to be found in the old Auberge d'Italie on Merchants Street. There are smaller branches in most other towns:

Sliema – Manwel Dimech Street.

St Julian's – Wilga Street, Paceville.

Gozo – 129 Republic Street, Victoria (Rabat); St. Anthony Street, Mġarr.

Postcards sent airmail to the UK cost 10c, and it is 12c to the USA and 16c to New Zealand. Stamps can also be bought at newsagents and hotels. High-quality commemorative stamps celebrating events in Malta's history are available from the Philatelic Bureau at the main post office in Valletta. A poste restante service is available at the main post office in Merchants Street, Valletta, Mon.-Fri. 0800-2000, Sat. 0800-1900. See **Opening Times**.

Public Holidays: 1 Jan. (New Year's Day); 10 Feb. (St. Paul's Shipwreck); 19 Mar. (St. Joseph's Day); 31 Mar. (Freedom Day); Good Friday; 1 May (May Day); 7 June (Sette Giugno); 29 June (Feast of St. Peter and St. Paul); 15 Aug. (Assumption); 8 Sep. (Our Lady of Victories); 21 Sep. (Independence Day); 8 Dec. (Immaculate Conception); 13 Dec. (Republic Day); 25 Dec. (Christmas Day). See FESTIVALS, **Religious Festivals**.

Rabies: The public health department is charged with keeping Malta rabies-free. Pets such as cats and dogs may be allowed in from the UK under strict supervision and subject to a minimum of three weeks in quarantine, but remember that you cannot take them back to the UK without incurring six months' quarantine.

Religious Festivals: The Maltese calendar is awash with religious festivals known as *festi*. Practically every weekend in summer there is one going on in one of the island's villages to celebrate a local saint's day. Everyone takes to the streets on the Saturday evening, there are fireworks and brass bands, and the church, streets and houses are specially decorated. The Sunday morning service will then be followed by a procession with a life-size statue of the saint concerned.

Of all the religious festivals, Easter is the most important: preparations begin weeks ahead. On Good Friday itself there are special church services at 1500 and solemn pageants recreating the Passion with statues being carried through the streets and followers dressed as Biblical characters. The atmosphere changes abruptly on Easter Sunday when *figolli* (special marzipan cakes in a pastry case shaped into fish and animals) are baked and blessed at early Mass, and people give chocolate birds and eggs to one another. Figures of the Risen Christ are then hoisted through the streets. See **FESTIVALS**, **Public Holidays**.

Religious Services:

Roman Catholic – Our Lady's Shrine, Mellieħa (1000 Sun.); St. Dominic's, Rabat (1115 Sun.); St. Paul's Chapel, St. Paul's Bay (1100 Sun.); St. Patrick's, St. John Bosco Street, Sliema (0730, 0900, 1000, 1930 Sun.); St. John of the Cross, Ta'Xbiex (1000 Sun.); Our Lady of Victories, Victory Square, Valletta (0900 Sun.); St. Joseph the Worker, Xemxija (1000 Sun.); Sacred Heart Seminary, Victoria (Rabat), Gozo (1000 Sun.); St. Paul's, Marsalforn (1100 Sun.); Our Lady of Mount Carmel, Xlendi (1000 Sun.); Comino Hotel, Comino (1630 Sat.).
Church of England – St. Paul's Anglican Cathedral, Independence Square, Valletta (Holy Communion 0800 Sun., 1000 Tue., Thu. & saints' days; Family Communion 1030 Sun.); Holy Trinity Church, Rudolphe Street, Sliema (Holy Communion 0800 Sun., 0930 Wed., Fri. & saints' days; sung Family Eucharist 1030 & Evensong).
Baptist Church – Filippo Sciberras Square, Floriana.
Church of Scotland/Methodist Church – St. Andrew's Church, corner of South Street and Old Bakery Street, Valletta.
Greek Orthodox Church – St. George, 83 Merchants Street (1000 Sun.).
Jewish services – contact Mr George Tayar, tel: 625717.

St. John's Co-Cathedral & Oratory:

Designed by Gerolamo Cassar (see **A-Z**), the building of this vast church for the Order of St. John was started in 1573. It is not easy to get a good view of the front because St. John Square is relatively small, but the plainness of the facade belies the extreme ornamentation inside. No surface remains uncarved, unpainted or ungilded. The floor is made up of intricate marble tombstones of the Knights of St. John (see **A-Z**) – coats of arms, cherubim, inscriptions, portraits, animals, birds and flowers are all created out of tiny pieces of coloured stone. Each side chapel is dedicated to a separate *langue* (language group) of the Order and contains the tombs of the Grand Masters. In the Oratory you will find Caravaggio's 1608 painting of *The Beheading of St. John*, and upstairs in the museum the 14 Flemish tapestries which are hung in the Cathedral during the feast of St. John in June. See **CHURCHES**, **MUSEUMS**, **Music**.

St. Paul (d. c. AD 76): It was under Roman rule that Christianity came to Malta with the arrival of Paul of Tarsus. After his conversion on the road to Damascus, Paul's preaching, which caused riots and disturbances of the peace in Jerusalem, became a thorn in the flesh of the city's Roman governor. Since Paul was a Roman citizen, he was allowed to appeal to the Roman emperor; so in AD 60 he was put on board a ship bound for Rome to face trial there. A fierce storm blew the ship onto the rocks at the mouth of what is known today as St. Paul's Bay (see **St. Paul's Island**), and the shipwrecked apostle was taken to meet the island's governor, Publius, who resided in a magnificent villa in the old capital of Melita, now thought to have occupied the site of Mdina's Cathedral. Paul succeeded in converting Publius to Christianity and is attributed with miraculously curing his father of illness. Paul possibly spent three months altogether on the island, living for the most part in the cave known as the Grotto of St. Paul in Rabat (see **ANCIENT SITES 2**), before being taken to Rome where he met his death and was eventually canonized. He spent much of his time on Malta preaching the Gospel, and is commemorated in churches and festivals throughout the islands for having brought the Word. See **FESTIVALS**.

St. Paul's Island (Selmunett): This is the spot where St. Paul (see **A-Z**) is traditionally supposed to have been shipwrecked in St. Paul's Bay. A statue of the saint dominates the island. See **Boat Trips**.

Sciortino, Antonio (1883-1947): The sculptor of the monument to the Great Siege of 1565 (see **A-Z**), which can be seen in Great Siege Square in Valletta. The three figures represent Courage, Liberty and Religion.

St Paul's Catacombs

Floriana

Senglea (L'Isla): Bus 3. Once one of the most densely populated areas of the island, much of the town was destroyed during World War II (see **A–Z**) and today Senglea's main claim to fame is in providing a marvellous viewpoint from which to appreciate the fortifications of Valletta and Vittoriosa (see **A–Z**). Like the latter, and Cospicua (see **A–Z**), this is one of the so-called 'three cities'. The waterfront is also an interesting area, with cafés, *dgħajjes* for hire (see **Water-taxis**) and ships coming and going in Dockyard Creek.

Shopping: Republic Street, running right down the centre of Valletta, together with its side streets, is the capital's main shopping area where you will find everything you might expect in a small capital city. There are branches of some of the international chains, such as Marks & Spencer, as well as souvenir shops (see **ARTS & CRAFTS**), boutiques, photographic suppliers and the usual run of chemists, banks, etc. The Tower Road area of Sliema also has a good selection of shops, with branches of many of the stores you will find in Valletta, such as The Leather Shop on Bisazza Street, as well as quite a few international chains like Benetton (junction of Tower Road and Bisazza Street), Pierre Cardin (Bisazza Street), the Body Shop (Tignè seafront), Bata (bottom of Bisazza Street) and Next (opposite Bata).
Shopping on Gozo is largely confined to the narrow streets of Victoria (Rabat), but you will also find roadside stalls selling knitwear and lace, and the villages of Xlendi and Marsalforn have souvenir shops. See **MARKETS, SHOPPING 1 & 2**, **Best Buys**, **Markets**.

Sliema: Bus 70 from Buġibba/St. Paul's Bay; Bus 60-64 from Valletta. See **WALK 2**.

Smoking: Smoking is prohibited on buses and in cinemas.

Sports: Sports complexes:
Marsa Sports Club, Marsa – tennis, squash, golf, archery.
Victoria (Rabat), Gozo – volleyball, basketball, handball, gymnastics, tennis, badminton, five-a-side football, squash, library, clinic.
Mistra Village Sports Centre, Mistra – indoor pool, gymnasium, saunas, squash, tennis.

Trim and Tonic Club, Galaxy Tourist Complex, Sliema – outdoor and indoor pools, Jacuzzi, gymnasium, sauna, squash.

Horse riding – Hal Ferh, tel: 473882/3, rides from Golden Bay (see **BEACHES 1**) to the Popeye Village (see **CHILDREN**). Costs Lm2 per hr; if you go for 2 hr they will pick you up from your hotel.

Tennis – Hilton Hotel, Dragonara Palace, Holiday Inn, Ta'Cenc (Gozo). Squash – Eden Beach Hotel, Holiday Inn, Atlas Hotel, Corinthia Hotel. Bowling – Eden Super Bowl, St. George's Bay, St. Julian's (1000-2400), computerized scoring, fast-food bar, air conditioning.

See **Water Sports**.

Taxis: Metered white taxis charge government-controlled rates. Black taxis with red number plates (first figure should be Y) are private and you can either rely on the meter price or agree a price for the journey before you set out. There are taxi ranks at several locations around town and outside hotels. You can also hail them in the street. A typical fare from the airport (see **A-Z**) to Sliema is around Lm5. Taxi drivers expect a tip (see **Tipping**).

Telephones & Telegrams: Public telephone booths are situated at the following Telemalta offices: Mercury House (main office), St. George's Road, St. Julian's (24 hr); South Street, Valletta (0800-1830 Mon.-Fri.); Luqa Airport (24 hr); Bisazza Street, Sliema (0830-2300); Qawra (0830-2300); Republic Street, Victoria (Rabat), Gozo (0800-2030 Mon.-Sat., 0800-1930 Sun.); and at the Police Station, Marsalforn, Gozo (24 hr).

To direct dial abroad, first dial 00 followed by the code for the country (UK – 44), then remember to omit the first 0 of the city code before dialling the rest of the number. All calls from Gozo should be preceded by an 8. If you want to make a person-to-person call, dial 994 (894 from Gozo) to get through to the Overseas Telephone Network. It is cheapest to telephone between 2100-0800.

Telegrams can be sent from all the above Telemalta offices or tel: 334042. Tel: 334045 for enquiries about received telegrams.

There are public Telex booths at St. Julian's, Valletta, Luqa and Victoria (Rabat). For the fax service, tel: 334041.

Television & Radio: Radio Malta One (999 KHz, 301 m MW) and Radio Malta Two (937 MHz VHF/FM), operated by the Telemalta Corporation, broadcast music, magazine and sports programmes as well as the news and weather in both English and Maltese. The BBC World Service is received clearly (wavelengths and listings in *The Times* – see **What's On**).
The local television channel is the commercial station, Television Malta (TVM). About half the programmes originate on the island and the rest are imported from the UK, Europe and the US.

Theatre: The delightful old Manoel Theatre, on the aptly named Old Theatre Street in Valletta, dates from 1731 and still puts on performances of music, drama and dance by local theatre groups, visiting artistes from all over the world, and the Manoel Symphony Orchestra. It is open for tours 1045 and 1130 Mon.-Fri. (50c). Seats cost upwards of Lm1.
The Astra Theatre on Republic Square in Victoria (Rabat), Gozo features productions by local groups as well as visiting shows and concerts from Malta and Europe. See **Cameras & Photography**, **Music**.

Time Difference: Two hours ahead of GMT in summer (last Sun. in Mar.-3rd Sun. in Sep.). One hour ahead of GMT in winter.

Tipping: It is customary to give taxi drivers and hairdressers a 10% tip, porters around 50c, and to leave an extra 10-15% in restaurants even when there is a cover charge.

Toilets: There is usually a clean toilet in even the smallest bar or café and public toilets are also well kept, though few and far between. It is as well to keep a supply of toilet paper or paper tissues with you.

Tourist Information: The head office of the National Tourism Organization is at Harper Lane, Floriana, tel: 224444/228282, and its main information office is at 1 City Gate Arcade, Valletta, tel: 227747. Branch offices are at Mġarr Harbour, Gozo, tel: 553343; Luqa Airport, tel: 229915; Balluta, St. Julian's, tel: 342671/2; and Bisazza Street,

Sliema, tel: 313409. The staff at these offices all speak English and are happy to provide information and help with accommodation, tours and excursions, car hire and official guides as well as any general assistance you may require. You will also be able to pick up useful leaflets and maps.

The Information Officer of the Malta National Tourist Office in the UK is at Mappin House, Suite 300, 4 Winsley Street, London W1N 7AR, tel: 071-323 0506. See **Accommodation**, **Events**, **Tours**, **What's On.**

Tours: Numerous companies organize day trips from Malta to Gozo, taking in the major sights and/or the best beaches (see BEACHES 2, EXCURSION 4, **Gozo**). Two of the best-known operators running these trips are Captain Morgan and Jylland, who also offer day trips to Comino (see **A-Z**). See **Boat Trips.**

Coach and minibus tours of Malta and Gozo can be arranged through Josephine's Booking Office, 80 The Strand, Sliema; Robert Arrigo & Sons Ltd, 12 Tagliaferro Centre, High Street, Sliema; and numerous small operators in Buġibba (e.g. T.C. Tours, Triq it-Trunciera) and St. Paul's Bay. In addition, many hotels offer their own bus tours, including trips to Valletta (see WALK 1, **A-Z**), Mdina (see WALK 3, **A-Z**), Gozo (see **A-Z**), the Blue Grotto (see **A-Z**), prehistoric temples (see ANCIENT SITES 1 & 2), the Ta Qali Craft Village (see ARTS & CRAFTS), the Popeye Village (see **CHILDREN**), Marsaxlokk (see EXCURSION 1) and several beaches (see BEACHES 1 & 2, **Bathing**). See **Tourist Information.**

Transport: Hiring a car is one of the best ways to get about on Malta and Gozo. Equipped with a good map (see **Orientation**), you can get to out-of-the-way sights and bathing places relatively quickly, avoiding the heat and slowness of crowded buses as well as long walks. See **Bicycle & Motorcycle Hire**, **Boat Trips**, **Buses**, **Car Hire**, **Ferries**, **Karrozzini**, **Water-taxis.**

Traveller's Cheques: See **Money.**

Triton Fountain: This huge fountain of bearded Tritons – half man, half fish – created by the Maltese sculptor Vincent Apap, stands right in the middle of the busy bus terminus outside City Gate in Valletta (see **Buses**). It is unfortunate that it is not often seen to be working.

University of Malta: Bus 60-64. The origins of Malta's university at Tal-Qroqq, Msida can be traced back to the 16thC. Today some 2000 students attend this historic institution which has some fine new buildings overlooking Msida. See **Cinemas**.

Valletta: The city of Valletta was built at the instigation of Grand Master de la Valette of the Order of St. John of Jerusalem after the Great Siege (see **A-Z**) of 1565, when the Turks were narrowly defeated and it was expected they might return at any time. The new city and its massive defences were designed by Francesco Laparelli, the Pope's architect and an assistant of Michelangelo's. Grand Harbour (see **FORTIFICATIONS**), one of the safest and most fought over natural harbours in the world, was used by the British (see **British Connection**) as a major naval base until 1979. See **WALK 1**.

Vittoriosa (Birgu): Bus 1, 2, 4, 6. Once just a little fishing village, this is where the Knights of St. John (see **A-Z**) originally set up residence when they first arrived from the island of Rhodes. Gradually they fortified the area and built Fort St. Angelo on the promontory. Several of their original seven great *auberges* (see **A-Z**) have survived here, and the Inquisitor's Palace on Main Gate Street now houses the National Museum of Folklore (0745-1400 mid June-Sep.; 0815-1700 Mon.-Sat., 0815-1615 Sun., Oct.-mid June; closed hol.). The town became known as Vittoriosa (Victorious) after the Great Siege (see **A-Z**), but you will find that many Maltese still refer to it as Birgu. Along with Senglea (see **A-Z**) and Cospicua (see **A-Z**), it is one of Malta's so-called 'three cities'. See **Markets**, **Water-taxis**.

Water Sports: Conditions for water sports are superb.
Diving – Strand Diving Services, John Zammit Street, Żebbuġ (school below the Gillieru Restaurant, Church Street, St. Paul's Bay); Divewise Services Ltd, Dragonara Water Sports Centre, St. Julian's.
Sailing – Valletta Yacht Club, Fort Manoel, Couvre Porte, Manoel Island, Gzira (welcomes members of overseas yacht clubs); Ghadira Sailing Club, PO Box 379, Valletta (organizes dinghy and sailboard racing); Malta Yachting Centre, Manoel Island Bridge, Gzira (yachts for hire).
Fishing – Small boats and fishing gear are available for hire in most locations (costs Lm9-Lm13 per day depending on size of boat, number in party, etc.). See **Bathing**, **Sports.**

Water-taxis: Pretty, brightly-painted *dgħajjes* cross from Valletta to Senglea (see **A-Z**) and Vittoriosa (see **A-Z**) in summer. Originally, these boats ferried crews ashore from visiting ships. Arrange the price before you leave. See **FESTIVALS**, **Boat Trips**.

What's On: The bi-weekly, English-language *What's On* guide is full of useful information on music and sporting events, art shows, drama programmes, special tours, exhibitions and festivals. The local daily newspaper, *The Times*, publishes cinema, television and radio programmes as well as details of sporting fixtures, musical attractions and advertisements for nightclubs, restaurants and excursions. Both publications are available from newsstands. Tourist offices (see **Tourist Information**) also provide information on events, festivals, etc. See **FESTIVALS**, **Events**, **Newspapers**.

World War II: Malta's strategic position placed it at the centre of the struggle for supremacy in the Mediterranean during World War II. Its isolation, on the other hand, meant that it was extremely difficult to defend, being only some 60 miles from Sicily (then enemy territory) and over 1000 miles from the nearest British base at Gibraltar. Lying directly in the path of communications between Italy and North Africa, its harbours and airfields became a convenient base from which to hamper the enemy. The bombing and second great siege of Malta began in 1940 but, despite this, the harbour continued to provide a haven and repair yard for Allied shipping, although it was hard to keep the supply route to the island open. By 1942 the Maltese people were in great need of food, fuel and medical supplies. In August a convoy finally got through and the turning point was reached.

The fortitude and assistance of the islanders was recognized by Britain, which awarded the George Cross 'to the island fortress of Malta to bear witness to a heroism and devotion that will long be famous in history', as the plaque on the Grand Master's Palace in Valletta (see **BUILDINGS, A-Z**) testifies. You can see the medal itself in the Fort St. Elmo War Museum (see **MUSEUMS, WALK 1**), together with photographs and memorabilia of the period. See **Air Force Memorial**.

Youth Hostels:

Marsaxlokk Hostel, Zejtun Road, tel: 871709 (70 beds, café).
St. Francis Ravelin Hostel, Floriana, tel: 224446 (80 beds, café).
Paceville Hostel, 30b Gale, Triq Wilga, Paceville, tel: 229361 (8 beds).
Trafalgar Hostel, 100 Triq ic-Centurjun, Buġibba, tel: 640412 (30 beds).
Youth Travel Circle Hostel, Buskett, Rabat, tel: 233893 (38 beds).
The Valletta Youth Hostels Association can be contacted at 17 Tal-Borg Street, Paola, tel: 229361, but is not affiliated in any way to the International Youth Hostels Association. To join you must be under 26 and membership costs Lm2.25.

This book was produced using QuarkXPress™
and Adobe Illustrator 88™ on Apple
Macintosh™ computers and output to separated
film on a Linotronic™ 300 Imagesetter

Text: Hilary Hughes
Photography: Phil Springthorpe
Electronic Cartography: Susan Harvey Design

First published 1991
Reprinted 1992 (twice)
Copyright © HarperCollins Publishers
Printed in Hong Kong
ISBN 0 00 435844-9